Also By
Dr. Sharon H. Porter
www.authordrsharonhporter.com

Next In line to Lead : The Voice of the Assistant Principal

Class of 2017! What's Next?

Women Who Lead: Extraordinary Women With Extraordinary Achievements Volume 1

Women Who Lead : Extraordinary Achievements With Extraordinary Achievements Volume 2 Featuring Latina Leaders

The Power of Networking: How to Achieve Success With Business Networking

North Carolina Girls Living In A Maryland World

Fifty & Fabulous The 2019 Edition

The HBCU Experience Anthology Volume 1 The North Carolina A&T State University Edition

The HBCU Experience Anthology Volume 2 Alumni Stories From the Hill of Kentucky State University

Women Who Lead

Extraordinary Women With Extraordinary Achievements

Volume 3

Featuring School Principals

Foreword by Dr. Essie McKoy

VISIONARY AUTHOR

Dr. Sharon H. Porter

Copyright © 2020 Perfect Time SHP LLC

All rights reserved. No portion of this book may be reproduced, stored in a retrieval system, or transmitted in any form or by any means—electronic, mechanical, photocopy recording, scanning, or other—except for brief quotations without the prior written permission of the publisher..

For information regarding special discounts for bulk purchases or purchases by organizations, associations, and nonprofits, please contact the publisher: **Perfect Time SHP Publishing.**

info@perfecttimeshp.com

www.perfecttimeshppublishing.com

Published by Write the Book Now, an imprint of Perfect Time SHP LLC.

ISBN-13: 978-1-734 7783-1-1

Contents

ACKNOWLEDGEMENTS i

Foreword 3

INTRODUCTION 7

Black. Girl. Leader. - Shelley Anderson 10

Can I Do This? - Dr. Shirley P. Auguste 24

You Know You Are a Principal, Right? My Journey to Principalship - D. JaMese M. Black 40

The Road Less Traveled - Kirsten Clark 53

Fearless Leadership - Tiawana Giles 64

Growth Is Mandatory - Natasha McDonald 72

Transforming School Culture: Toxic to Tolerable, to Teamwork - Lydia Ryan 94

Work-life Balance - Dr. Amy Miller 106

Leaps of Faith - Amena Moiz 116

I am Enough Charlene Saenz-Quarles 129

Purpose: You Can Run, But You Can't Hide - Danielle Wallace . 139

ACKNOWLEDGEMENTS

I would like to thank the contributing authors of Women Who Lead Volume 3 Featuring School Principals for sharing their leadership journey:

Shelly Anderson

Dr. Shirley P. Auguste

D. JaMese Morris Black

Kirsten Clark

Tiawana Giles

Natasha McDonald

Lydia Ryan Menzer

Dr. Amy Miller

Amena Moiz

Charlene Saenz-Quarles

Danielle Wallace

Foreword

Visionary Author, Dr. Sharon H. Porter executed the vision of bringing together women of all nationalities, ethnic groups, social classes, and levels of experience to share their leadership stories in the field of education.

Women Who Lead: Extraordinary Women with Extraordinary Achievements, Featuring School Principals is a compilation of practicing principals' leadership successes and challenges. These women leaders are from all levels of school administration and from many locations throughout the United States.

The contributing authors focused on sharing authentically about their own journey so that others could learn and gain practical strategies to apply to their leadership toolkit, as well as provide insights to help guide those aspiring to become leaders of tomorrow. They share in order to be a support and provide guidance for aspiring principals. Their wealth of knowledge is impactful not only to those desiring to maximize their skills and invest in themselves, but it will impact many generations to come as they pass the torch from one extraordinary woman to the next!

These leaders share their mountaintop successes to deep valley challenges about what it took to get to where they are today and how they were able to create opportunities out of their struggles in leadership. They share the glaring moments of their individual and collective successes. Highly effective leaders will tell you that they had to build a great team to reach the pinnacle of success. They did not arrive there alone!

No matter how great one may be, it takes a highly effective team to move the needle in education. I can assure you that these teams of educators created by these extraordinary women owned the vision of making an impact. They believed in something that was greater than themselves and their convictions guided their work.

In this best-selling book, each woman provided their experience from their perspective, from their understanding of what led to their present day role and their successes, and what it will take to continue the journey of excellence as they serve and make a systemic difference in the lives of students and educators.

To do the work that they have done, they had to be passionate, insightful, self-aware, possessors of inner strength, resourceful, keen listeners, strategic in their approach, inspiring to those they led, promoters of team building and establishers of positive relationships, seekers of innovation and creativity, optimistic, confident, life-long learners, effective communicators, accountable, goal oriented, persist in spite of challenges, manage complex tasks and a multitude of responsibilities, hold an unlimited vision, and believe in children and educators! Their successes were not driven by their own desire to be great, but their desire to serve others, to give back, to make a change, and to help students reach the next level to achieving their dreams.

These phenomenal women made personal sacrifices to serve! They had to sometimes be absent in the lives of their own children, miss important functions, and balance their leadership responsibilities to continue the journey of serving. The road to being a great leader is filled with many sacrifices and a multitude of internal emotions of wanting to be the greatest, but ensuring your own personal needs are not in conflict with your professional responsibilities.

Many times, they stretched their capacity and honed their skills to be great leaders. There were times when they faced insurmountable challenges in which they had to recharge and be even more strategic in their approach. You will be amazed at reading about their experiences and walking through the lives of such outstanding women leaders.

Their stories are inspiring and filled with genuineness about their triumphs and their struggles. Any educator can tell you that the task of educating our future is a tremendous responsibility! Often, it lies on the shoulders of school leaders! It is often stated that school leadership can be a lonely journey, but each leader must decide and operate from their core and this determines whether they embrace others on the journey or walk the journey alone. While everyone is a stakeholder and makes great contributions to the overall betterment of educating our student, the one person with whom everyone looks to for answers, for results, for tough decisions, and for propelling the vision forward is the school leader. These women have proven themselves repeatedly in answering the call and doing the work! They were able to balance the woes of leadership while navigating the school to a level beyond what they had already achieved.

These women were comprehensive in their leadership style, encompassing "the whole child, the whole school, and the whole educator." Interestingly, it is sometimes a challenge for these leaders to see the long-range magnitude of their systemic impact while serving, but through their stories, you can feel how their vision reaches wide and their mission serves expansively.

Women Who Lead: Extraordinary Women with Extraordinary Achievements, Featuring School Principals cannot be overlooked! These leaders share how to lead with courage and share how you can be the best leader that you can possibly be! You read the pages and feel that there is so much greatness even in your own untapped potential. The leadership stories bring to life the leader in you. Learning from these EXTRAORDINARY women will only elevate your leadership journey, expand your capacity, and broaden your depth of knowledge.

Dr. Essie McKoy President, CEO, and Founder, Dr. Essie Speaks, LLC

INTRODUCTION

The Women Who Lead Book Series was created to simply serve as a guide to young girls and younger women finding their place in society.

Women Who Lead Featuring School Principals *details the journey of new and experienced principals as they make their mark in their school community. The principalship is challenging while at the same time rewarding. Principals work tirelessly to serve their school community, oftentimes with little appreciation.*

Leadership is second to only to teaching in its impact on student success according to the landmark study, How Leadership Influences Student Learning. *As a principal, we observe classrooms, provide professional development, create and maintain a culture for teaching and learning, work to build positive relationships with stakeholders, all while focusing on the instructional core, teachers, students, and content.*

Principals are vital to the successful implementation of instruction. They must be data-driven in order to improve student achievement. Data plays an integral role in decision-making.

I became a principal for the first time in 2008. I was employed in a large urban school district in the Washington DC metropolitan area. While excited I also was unsure of the road ahead. I survived my first year only because of a close knit group of colleagues... self-

identified as the "Dream Team". The Dream Team consisted of several first year principals and one principal who had served in the role one or two years more than the rest of us. We met weekly and held true to not reinventing the wheel. We shared everything. It made our first year successful. After two years as principal at an elementary school, I was asked to transfer to a middle school that was having challenges. The principal was being removed and new (different) assistant principals would also be sent to the school. I accepted this challenge, as I had a special love for middle school. Here I was, now a "new" principal to middle school. That same year, a family situation would have me resign my position in that school district and return to my home state of North Carolina. I was fortunate enough to be hired as a middle school principal in North Carolina, the school district in which I attended and graduated. "I am a new principal again, this time, in a new school district and a new state. It was quite a different experience as I was the first African-American principal the school had and the first female African-American in the town where the school was located. New experiences, new learning, and new perspectives.

After two and half years, I was able to return back to the Washington, DC area. Again, I was fortunate to be hired back in the school district I left. This time, I served as principal in a public charter school on Joint Base Andrews, in Maryland. Although I was familiar with the school district, the newness was charter school and working directly with military families. I gained so much new experience serving at this location. I served on this campus for one school year, before I began serving as a Leadership Development Coach, working with first and second year assistant principals and principals. This was one of the most enjoyable, rewarding, positions I had held in education to date. So enjoyable in fact, that I made a decision to go back to the schoolhouse as a building principal so I would be able to start my own leadership development program through my coaching firm, Perfect Time SHP LLC. The Next In Line to Lead Aspiring Principal Leadership Academy was born July

INTRODUCTION

2019. I now get to lead a school while also coaching and mentoring aspiring principals from across the United States. This book was written specifically with aspiring and new principals in mind.

As an aspiring or new principal, you first must know that a mentor, coach, and/or support group is needed. Having help does not signal weakness, but it is a sign of wisdom and strength. It shows your commitment for continued improvement. Research-based evidence reveals that quality mentoring relationships result in many career-enhancing benefits (Principal Magazine 2013). Making the Case for Principalship Mentoring, *a report published by NAESP and the Education Alliance at Brown University, contends that principals are traditionally "thrown into their jobs without a lifejacket", unprepared for the demands of the position, feeling isolated and without guidance.*

I encourage you, if your district does not assign a mentor and a development coach to you as a new principal or aspiring principal, be your own advocate and find someone to assist you in navigating these leadership waters. It is quite a journey, but one that will bring fulfillment if you have appropriate guidance.

Learn from the lessons of these extraordinary school principals. Reach out to them with questions as you build your network of mentors and coaches.

Shelley Anderson

We can, whenever and wherever we choose, successfully teach all children whose schooling is of interest to us. We already know more than we need to do that. Whether or not we do it must finally depend on how we feel about the fact that we haven't so far."
- Ron Edmonds

CHAPTER 1

BLACK. GIRL. LEADER.

By Shelley Anderson

"Our deepest fear is not that we are inadequate. Our deepest fear is that we are powerful beyond measure. It is our light, not our darkness that most frightens us."
– Marrianne Williamson

At an early age my mother instilled in me a love for reading, and a deep curiosity about the world. We would sit together and explore new worlds of animals, space creatures, and pernicious children eager to embark on wild adventures. As an only child, I rarely felt lonely because there were always fresh adventures waiting for me in a book. At the time I was unaware how much an early grasp of literacy and an appreciation for reading would serve me in the future. My parents, both full-time ministers, also instilled in me at an early age the value of leading a life of service. There in a small, rural Kansas town, we were frequently involved in missionary service, assisting those in need, and speaking life into people who fell on hard times. As I watched my parents give so freely of their time and energy, I learned that true happiness comes from serving others.

By the time I started school I was reading and writing well above grade level, and therefore spent most of my time watching the other kids, a unique opportunity for an only child used to being surrounded by adults. Although I did not struggle academically, there were times when I suffered socially. At the time, my parent's missionary service had led us to a small town in rural Kansas. I attended an elementary campus where I was the only person of color. My braided pigtails smelled of fresh coconut oil, and my face was the color of a roasted almond. I stuck out like a sore thumb. Most teachers and students were 'kind'. The third-grade girls made me their baby doll, carrying me around on the playground, catering to my every wish. It was the equivalent of kindergarten royalty, even though I secretly felt some shame in the 'honor' when I saw that my fairer-skinned peers were not played with as a doll. The teachers delved out their own brand of 'kindness', making sure I was line leader on MLK Day, but without possibility of leading on any other day . The 'kindness' may have been tainted but it was nothing compared to the meanness. Some kids told me that they weren't allowed to touch me because I may get them dirty. Others held their nose when I passed them in the hallway. In first grade Phillip told the others that I smelled bad because I was a "N". I was shocked because I thought he was my friend and I didn't 'know' that I was a "N", or that I smelled. This new knowledge left me insecure and wounded. I stopped answering questions that I knew the answer to. I sat alone at lunch. I practiced disappearing.

By the time Stacy, another little girl of color, moved into our classroom I wanted nothing to do with her. She was loud, "just like a 'N'", according to Phillip, and she didn't comb her hair. I overheard a teacher say that she came because of some new apartments that had been built. She continued with a warning, "there will be more".

In 1988 we moved to Texas from Kansas, to assist with a small congregation on the Texas-Oklahoma border that needed my parent's help. The schools in Texas were more diverse, and there were special programs for students, like myself, who were identified as Gifted. I met many educators who saw my potential and spent unrequired time providing encouragement. One such blessing was my sixth-grade G/T teacher, Ms. Wesson. She always pushed us to think at higher levels, ask questions that challenged what was known, and make connections between major events in world history and current events. She recognized that I seemed to be very good at making connections. She decided to name me 'world correspondent' and give me time to update the entire G/T class about world events. I'm not sure if she knew how much confidence the opportunity gave me. How could she have known? I happened to be the only girl of color in the classroom, and this time I was different because I was a leader.

My Path to Educational Leadership

"We ask ourselves, Who am I to be brilliant, gorgeous, talented, fabulous? Actually, who are you not to be? You are a child of God. Your playing small does not serve the world."-**Marriane Williamson**

When I first started teaching, I thought I would change the world! And, in some ways I did.

However, my students have done much more for me than I ever did for them. They made me more aware, more alive. They made me a leader.

I took an untraditional route to the classroom. In college, I changed majors four times, took a year off to live in Europe, and when I finally emerged with a degree, was still hopelessly unclear on what I actually wanted to do. I didn't have the gall to tell my mother that 'wandering poet' was under consideration, so the third time she asked, I casually mentioned teaching. I had already received my first experience with teaching in Europe, where I held a part-time job teaching Italian teens English. I had received very little direction from the organization that hired me, and in less than a week I was ushered into a classroom full of pubescent young Romans more anxious to learn about my American life than the monotonous rules of the English language. It was an instant love affair. Pleasant memories of fun afternoons full of laughter, earnest inquiries regarding the Real Slim Shady, and Italian sodas sealed my decision, and one month later I was in an alternative certification program. Six months later, I had my own classroom.

My young adulthood mirrored my teaching career, a time of discovery that led to rich new experiences. Personally, I held a new found freedom and responsibility living alone in the middle of a big city, discovering new cuisine, art, music, and love. In the same way my classroom became a creative Launchpad for ways to increase student understanding. Sometimes I would teach the same lesson, six different ways, changing variables for every group of students who entered my room. The creative license was hypnotic and I soon became mesmerized with finding unique ways to assist students in mastering difficult concepts. I turned a lesson on Newton's 3 laws into a soccer game on the patio where every athletic action had to be accompanied by shouting out the corresponding law it explained. Chemistry lessons became opportunities to make ice cream in plastic bags and shoot rocket ships powered by Alka-Seltzer tablets, the water cycle, a chance to make a rap video. My district Benchmark test scores showed that the students were learning Science, and I was learning that creative problem-solving is a must for effective leadership.

The lessons didn't just end with instruction. Our campus was in the middle of a mostly minority neighborhood devastated by crime, poverty, and drug use. The students were testaments to the best and worst in the community. I listened to their stories of bravely traveling to a new country and their shock of being received into overcrowded homes shared by multiple families who had made the same journey and were now crammed into the same holding pattern.

I listened to their stories of abuse, sometimes due to violent alcoholic or drug addicted parents, sometimes due to the greed of an adult intent on stealing their innocence, always heartbreaking. I also listened to the pride in their voices as they described their families, their culture, the dreams that they shared with their parents of a brighter future. As I listened, I internalized both their pain and their hope, and I learned that leadership requires the ability to listen and empathize with others.

My third year in teaching began with a financial crisis in my district that led to an immediate RIF (reduction in force). Although I kept my job, I watched our campus descend into paranoia as they speculated on who would be cut, who would remain, who was worthy, who was not. In the end, we lost 7 staff members, a mix of teachers, para-professionals, and support staff sacrificed to the gods of poorly written state and district policies. The RIF was my first experience of education policy gone wrong. Money was tight for the rest of the year. Class sizes increased, while accountability remained the same. Our newly appointed principal didn't appreciate my flare for creative lessons, or my focus on building student relationships. Her focus was test scores. And her focus did not include a holistic look at improving student outcomes. She wanted higher TAKS scores and she wanted them immediately. There wasn't any training provided on how to produce these higher scores, just lots of talk about people losing their jobs if they didn't produce. Morale plummeted as the initial fear of unemployment gave way to anger. The school I loved began to suffer under tyrannical leadership, and I learned that poor leadership is the quickest way to ruin any organization.

Although I was disheartened by the current circumstance, I began to reflect on some of my most inspiring students in an effort to remember my motivation for becoming an educator. Students who against all odds excelled in a new country, with a new language, to become the first member of their family to not only graduate from high school but also attend college. Students who attended school every day, with a smile, even when their lights were off at home and the refrigerator was empty. Students who laughed when most would have cried and shrugged when most would have screamed. Students who chose to persevere instead of giving up. And I realized that I must use their strength, to find my own! I realized that true leaders stay and fight when others run. I finished the school year, and even stayed and served as the Science Department chair the following year.

Right before my fifth year of teaching, my former principal, Dr. Arias, contacted me with an opportunity to move to her campus and serve as the AVID (Advancement Via Individual Determination) teacher and coordinator. I was familiar with the AVID program and wholly aligned with its determination to close the achievement gap by giving all students the skills that they needed to attend, and graduate from a four-year university. During this time my principal invested in me by building both my content knowledge, and my leadership experience. She had me present to the entire faculty on a frequent basis to demonstrate the benefits of the AVID program. She also gave me the flexibility to manage my site team of teachers, the program budget, the hiring of tutors, and the planning of all field trips. She met with me bi-weekly and asked me to reflect on the work I had done since our previous meeting. She always prompted me to think deeply about ways to grow as both a teacher and as a leader. Most importantly she taught me that the best leaders take pride in the development of other leaders.

Things were changing in my personal life as well. My campus leadership role led me to pursue a Master's degree in Curriculum and Instruction with a focus in Secondary Literacy. I was thrilled with the possibility of sharing my love of teaching and learning in an official role. My love life was looking up too. I met my husband, a handsome young engineer, when I tried recruiting him as a guest speaker for my AVID students. We were soon married, and we relocated to an area closer to his job. I was unsure what my future held, but certain that I would find a great school to continue teaching. As I followed my new husband on our journey to start a new life together, I realized that the best leaders also make the best followers.

When I went to interview for a teaching position at a middle school they offered me the position of Literacy Coach instead. They felt that my personality, experience, and current work on my Master's made me a perfect fit for the position. I was unsure of what being a campus instructional coach actually involved, but I was excited about being challenged by a new experience. My first year as a CIC was difficult. The teachers weren't as excited to hear about new strategies and resources as I had imagined. They took my suggestions as insults to their work. Instead of giving up, I decided to try a different approach. After reading a book about coaching, I decided to spend time building relationships and providing support. I would walk around every morning, say hello, and ask how I could help them have a better day. Teachers started to look forward to my visits, and soon started to seek me out to ask for my insights. From this experience I learned that building relationships is essential to gaining the trust and earning the respect of any team. As a team, we worked together to build campus wide literacy, drastically increase STAAR (The State of Texas Assessments of Academic Readiness) scores, and earn a state distinction in Reading.

In 2014, I received the leadership promotion of my life. I became a mother! On Valentine's Day I gave birth to a beautiful little boy named Trey Anderson. From the moment he arrived I felt an unparalleled sense of both love and responsibility. It also changed my commitment to education. I thought of Trey when I interacted with every child. Every interaction became an opportunity, a chance to shape a life for the better.

My zeal for school turnaround next led me to accept a central office job as an Academic Facilitator. The role involved me directly providing literacy support for 14 campuses, including 3 which had been labeled "IR". It was a fast-paced, intense position which required combining everything I knew about curriculum and instruction with everything I knew about leadership. It also gave me a unique opportunity to learn, as I worked directly with the Assistant Superintendent, 4 Executive Directors, and many principals and assistant principals. I observed educational leadership at its very best, and at times, at its worst. I joined side-by-side with principals who were in a fight to save their campus and we worked as a team to move 2 of the 3 "Improvement Required" rated campuses to a rating of "Met Standard". The experience taught me that real leaders fight as hard as they love, and that if you fight hard enough, you can and will win!

An old friend from my first years of teaching, called me quite unexpectedly at the end of August to offer me assistant principal at a large comprehensive high school in the famed south Dallas neighborhood known as Oak Cliff. My faith in public education had been shaken as I watched long-time friends in central office fall victim to district politics. It hurt to watch people who I had grown to love, people who had given so much of themselves in this work, being tossed aside as a new regime of district administration took control of our battered city. I was sickened by the constant political posturing while the lives of children continued to weigh in the balance and found wanting. It was time for me to be back on a campus full time to remember the love that kept me in this profession.

As an assistant principal, I had the privilege of watching a new generation of young teachers teach and learn their own lessons as they balanced the joys and challenges of life with the joys and challenges of the classroom. After my first year on the campus, we celebrated as our campus came together as a team to earn 7 out of 7 state distinctions. But the victories did not come without painful and hard lessons. I daily interacted with teens who found it normal to fully parent not only their younger brothers and sisters, but also their drug-addicted mothers and fathers who depended on them. I worked with students, who were restricted by ankle bracelets and monitored by probation officers. I witnessed the devastation on the faces of my mostly Latino student body on a cold day in November when they arrived at school heavy with the announcement that their dreams would soon be in the hands of a soon to be elected President Trump. My three years as an AP gave me the chance to listen as much as I spoke, and learn as much as I led. These lessons would soon be necessary for the trials of leadership that lay ahead.

My Current Situation

"And as we let our own light shine, we unconsciously give other people permission to do the same. As we are liberated from our own fear, our presence automatically liberates others."
-Marrianne Williamson

I am now a second year principal in charge of an urban middle school nestled amidst the hustle and bustle of Washington DC's Columbia Heights neighborhood. If you know DC well, then you probably know that Columbia Heights looks entirely different than it did as recently as five years ago. My school is one of these differences, set atop a CVS, and across from a new, shiny shopping conglomerate. We are part of a gentrification effort that feels finished, yet incomplete. The students who attend my school travel there from all of the eight DC wards. All are minorities, most live in severe poverty, and more than you would imagine are either homeless or in foster care. During my first week of school one of my eighth grade girls pulled me to the side to ask if I could make an exception for the knife she wished to carry in her backpack. She looked so small as she told me that she needed it to feel safe traveling to and from school every day. I stood silent, as I contemplated the enormity of her request, her need to feel safe, protected, and powerful enough to traverse the realities of her life, and what it demanded of her in order to make it to school; she needed me to make a real change.

My team and I have been able to make some strides in the year and a half that I have set as the leader of this campus. Even with limited resources we still have positively impacted both the students and the community we serve. We currently boast one of the most diverse student bodies in the city with about half of our students identified as "at-risk" and a third of our students identified as English Language Learners. We were recently recognized as one of a handful of secondary campuses in the city to be named a "Leveler school" because of our outstanding results with closing the gap in achievement for at-risk students. We currently have a 3 STAR rating which meets or exceeds the STAR rating for all other Ward 1 middle schools. In addition, last year, 100% of our 8th-grade students successfully navigated the complicated DC lottery system with ALL gaining acceptance to one of their choice high schools, and nearly half of those 8th-grade students being accepted to selective or Tier-1 Schools. However, we still have much work to do to ensure that all of our students truly have equitable access to an education that will change their lives for the better.

My Future- Leading Change

"You have to act as if it were possible to radically transform the world. And you have to do it all the time."

-Angela Davis

I now know that my destiny is to lead change in education. The traditional, American school experience fails to give equitable opportunities to all students, as it inherently favors the privileged few—affluent, Caucasian, straight male--over the many (everyone else). As an urban school principal who daily bears witness to the failures, I am convinced that there must be a complete restructuring of the system to celebrate and nurture the academic, social, emotional, and spiritual needs of each individual student is a moral imperative. Our only path forward, is to learn who our students are, the unique set of rules that governs each of their lives, and what they need to be successful. To meet those needs we need to personalize the experience of every student who walks through our doors.

Personalization, a business strategy developed to improve customer satisfaction and garner more sales, now thoroughly permeates almost every sector of society with the exception of education. The modern consumer thinks very little of making elaborate customized coffee orders, wearing self-created signature lip colors or tennis shoes, or updating their Instagram story, the ultimate idolatry of self, several times a day. With inexpensive, convenient DNA sequencing services like 23andMe offering personal wellness recommendations, the practice of medicine is already set on a revolutionary journey defined by who the patient is from head to… genome. Of course there have been glimpses of personalized learning in Pk-12 schools across the nation. Most have been confined to software programs that assess student academic progress, and then provide personalized e-lessons targeted to improve areas of growth. Although helpful, real practitioners understand lasting change is dependent on demolishing the current system of education in its entirety, and creating a new system anchored by the need of the individual student. Every student, a unique combination of talent, aspiration, personality, race, class, family dynamic, resilience and often, trauma, must be educated in a system that seeks to know who they already are, and believes that true education occurs only when the individual can synthesize knowledge of themselves, and knowledge of the world to lead fulfilling personal lives, and make meaningful contributions to society.

About Shelley Anderson

Shelley Anderson is a middle school principal in Northwest Washington, DC who has spent the past 15 years fighting to ensure that all students have equitable access to a rigorous and engaging curriculum. Her campus was recently named the only "Leveler" Ward One DC Middle School by the DC Policy Center, a distinct honor that means it is one of a handful of DC public schools to close the achievement gap and get positive results with at-risk youth.

Before relocating from Dallas, Texas to Virginia, she was an assistant principal in inner-city, mostly minority high school in Dallas. During her time there the campus earned 7 out of 7 distinctions from the state of Texas for outstanding academic achievements, and she was named Dallas ISD AVID Assistant Principal of the Year.

In addition, she has experience as an educational consultant, central office academic facilitator, campus literacy coach, and as a secondary Science, ELA, and AVID teacher. Shelley was a part of the 2017 and 2019 Harvard Graduate School of Education Urban School Leaders Cohorts and was the 2019 Greater Washington Urban League Election Committee Chair. She also was a 2018 Stanford University School Re-Tool Fellow.

Her deepest passion is being a mother to her brilliant, five year old son, Trey, who is on the Autism Spectrum.

SHELLEY ANDERSON

Dr. Shirley P. Auguste

"Leadership and learning are indispensable to each other."

-John F. Kennedy

CHAPTER 2

CAN I DO THIS?

By: Dr. Shirley P. Auguste

I am a first generation Haitian-American, Black-Hispanic, strong-willed woman. I am one of the first in my family to earn a college degree and the first on the maternal side to earn a doctorate degree. As a minority, education was important in my family. My parents and my aunt always told me that I had to go to college. Granted, I had no clue how to get to college—knowing that an education was important simply was not enough. However, I was blessed, because God brought a teacher into my life who opened the door and showed me how to complete the application and apply for financial aid. From that point on, however, it was up to me to do the work. I started off at Piedmont Community College and earned an Associate of Science in "General Studies" because I just did not know what to do or what direction I was supposed to take. When I transferred to Virginia Commonwealth University, I changed my major three times. My mother suggested I become a teacher "since I was good with children." My initial response was, "absolutely not! Teachers do not make any money." I was constantly reminded by my parents and my aunt to finish, so I knew I had to get a degree—

but I did not know what path to choose. A simple phone call kept me on track. My aunt called me and asked, "when are you going to get that diploma?" I was also reminded that everything I did would impact the younger generation. It was my responsibility to set a good example and make sure I became a positive role model. I worked different part-time jobs and focused on graduating.

When I first began my education, becoming an administrator was not a part of my agenda or dream. The reality is I did not know what it meant to be a school leader or administrator. My knowledge of different careers was limited to the medical field, engineering, law, military, religious leadership, and service positions such as barber, cosmetologist, mechanic, and working at a fast food restaurant. This might seem "unreal," to you that this was the limit of my knowledge, but it was the reality. It was not until I began to work as a teacher that I started to learn about leadership roles and the many different opportunities within the school system. As I learned, I began to observe leaders in the school system to try and figure out their role. It became very apparent to me that there were not many strong-willed Black-Hispanic women in school systems—let alone any Haitian women.

Needless to say, this journey of realization and discovery has not been easy. It was a lot harder than I could have ever imagined or expected. There were times I wondered if I should even continue pursuing a position as an administrator. There was always the question, "Can I do this?" There was no evidence that said, "yes you can." But for some reason, there was something in me that would not allow me to quit. An inner voice that reminded me of all of the obstacles I had experienced in life and the lack of self-confidence I had as a result. This led me to remember all of the children and their families out there who had experienced challenges that would hinder them from being motivated to pursue higher degrees. I also kept in mind the schools that were closing. There were families out there who wanted the same thing for their children that my family wanted for me, but they would not be able to get a good education for their children. Every family, despite their race, financial status, religion, or culture deserves the ability to provide a great education for their children. Children need to learn about the different careers open to them.

Learning about different careers happens in a school with teachers who love children, want to teach, and want to make a positive difference. Teaching in an impoverished area is not for just anyone. The education field is not just a job, it is a life of servitude and one that deserves much respect for the sacrifices that are made by educators. I loved being a teacher because of how much fun I could have with the students and how I was able to help them to learn to love learning. It was hard work constantly trying to learn new strategies to teach children that were two or three grade levels behind. However, I refused to allow any child to leave my class below grade level. I sacrificed my time and my own children's time to plan lessons and activities that would capture the children's attention while they were learning. And each year, I was satisfied, knowing that I gave my all to students and their families, most of them finishing above grade level or less than half a year below grade level. Unfortunately, I did not realize how great the sacrifice was that I was making. The sacrifice was time with my own children.

While a teacher in a certain district, I was able to see families changed and children excel because they learned the importance of their education through having fun and being able to relate to the content that was being taught. As a first generation Haitian-American, Black-Hispanic woman and one of the first in my family to go to college, being a teacher was never just a job. It became a passion to reach and help as many children and their families as I could to get a good education and learn how to go further in life. It was through this passion that I realized I wanted to do more and wanted to impact more children. Most of all, I wanted to give back.

Being a teacher, team leader, or coordinator of different tutoring programs was never enough for me because I was not reaching or helping enough children. There is a great need to touch as many lives as possible in impoverished areas such as urban or rural districts. I began to plan and dream of working as an administrator of a school, and I ultimately pursued an administrative degree.

At that time, I spoke to two of my mentors, Mr. and Mrs. Charles S. Brabble, Sr. and they told me that it would not be easy, but they encouraged me to pursue the administrative degree and reminded me to stay humble, keep God first and do everything in the best interest of the children. Mr. Charles S. Brabble, Sr. and Mary Brabble (deceased) were educators. They are legacies as educators. Mr. Brabble was supposed to work as an "intern principal," but was immediately placed as a principal. Mary Brabble was a "Home Economics" teacher. Both of them had a powerful impact on many lives in the school system where they taught. Mr. Brabble spent all of his years as an impactful administrator who changed lives and supported upcoming educators. Coming from a family of educators and having a wife that was in education, it was apparent that their lives were dedicated to educating the young and all those that were willing to listen and learn. I have been fortunate to have the opportunity to get counsel and words of wisdom from them on how to lead. It just required that I listen and follow through on the advice given.

As an educator, when I faced different challenges, I would call or go and visit the Brabbles. As a teacher, Mrs. Brabble usually had an answer for me. If she didn't, she would call on Mr. Brabble to give me advice. She was one of the most remarkable and strong black woman educators I knew. As I pursued my administrative degree, they became my primary "go to" for guidance. I asked questions and was intrigued by both of their stories. I always questioned, "Can I do this? Am I doing a good job or doing enough?" Over the years, I enjoyed listening to the stories and still seek guidance from Mr. Brabble. When I first began my experiences as a leader, Mr. Brabble gave me this advice:

1) *Keep God first in all you do and never go into the school building without praying for guidance*

2) *Be silent, listen, and get to know the relationships in your building*

3) *Keep your hands off the money*

4) *Always keep the students' best interest first*

5) *Treat people the way you want to be treated*

6) *Follow the policies and procedures*

These have become my guiding principles. I am grateful for his wisdom and continued guidance through any self-doubt, issues, or challenges I faced.

The people who have had the most profound impact on my life as a school leader were Mr. Charles S. Brabble, Sr and Mary Brabble (deceased). Even today, Mr. Brabble challenges me to strive to do more and be better. It is an honor to know that there is a legend who believes in me and is willing to continue to push me. During times of trials and extreme difficulties, when I feel as if I am failing the children because I am broken or have become weak, he encourages me and reminds me of how great I am. I could never describe how important that is to me. Life as a minority leader, especially a Black-Hispanic Haitian strong-willed woman, is beyond challenging. The challenges I've faced can and have shaken my self-esteem. I am blessed to have the Brabbles, my children, parents, family, educators, and friends who stand by and encourage me through these challenges.

As a leader, there are many times you will be knocked down. It is during these times that you have to know who to turn to for prayer, a self-esteem boost, and a pep talk. No one can succeed on their own. A leader can only be great thanks to the people around them that will pray, support, encourage, and uplift them in the good and challenging times. When I am weak and feel beaten down, I call on Mr. Brabble so I can listen to his stories. Those stories encourage and humble me, and make me ask myself, "How can I not push forward when a legend believes in me? He was an educator and has impacted so many." Like him, I can only push forward and strive to leave a mark wherever I go and in everything I do. I will always keep God first when I go into the school building and keep the children's best interest first. As I continue to grow and prosper as an administrator, I will continue to seek Mr. Brabble's advice and enjoy the lessons I learn from his stories. While I push forward, I will always remember and appreciate those who have stood with me, including my children, parents, best friend, Colonel Brown, my brother and his wife, sisters and their husbands, and my professors (Dr. Koonce, Dr. Clark, and Dr. Matthews). For this, I am beyond grateful for those that have supported me on my journey to become a school leader.

As a school leader, I am often called to make important decisions. Some of those decisions are:

1. *Creating a new vision, mission and values with the leadership team to provide direction of where I saw the staff and students in ten years. I wanted everyone to know we were going to be building life-long and continuous learners.*

2. *Being a positive role model for the staff and students on a daily basis by dressing professionally, smiling (no matter what I was facing), encouraging every student and staff I encountered, and being visible daily.*

3. *Dealing with cafeteria duty and everything with scheduling.*

4. *Reviewing data with staff or personally to study and determine areas needing support.*

5. *Delegating and trusting.*

6. *Remaining impartial. For example, when a teacher writes a student up, I have to remember to investigate to get the facts and come up with a consequence that follows the Student Code of Conduct and that will not have a detrimental impact on the student's desire to learn or want to be in school. I have learned that just because a student is "written up" does not mean that the write up is justifiable. Being an administrator means I must be impartial in order to do the right thing for the student, staff, and school.*

7. *Accepting that I was not always going to be liked and everyone would not agree with me. This can be a huge challenge. I used to think this was an easy task, until I was in that position as school principal, and I was faced with several challenges that were out of my control. No matter what I did, I was faced with obstacles and pushback. The key was to continue moving forward, doing the right thing, treating everyone with respect and dignity, being a professional, remembering why I was there and continuing to encourage myself. As an administrator, you are not always going to be liked and that is "Ok." It is important to maintain a level of professionalism and not cross the line into friendship with a colleague. This can cloud your judgement, people will get hurt, and fairness will disappear. To be successful, it is important to be fair.*

8. *Remembering the number of negative or challenging people are very minor compared to the number of amazingly wonderful, dedicated and hard-working staff members. The good might be silent but they always outweigh the negative. Stay focused on them.*

9. *Continuously work towards building a positive, rigorous, and collaborative environment by determining who were my "silent leaders." I enlisted their help while working with the leadership team to create an environment that I would be proud to bring my own children.*

10. *Always remembering the children are the reasons I am in this profession and they deserve the best of the best in education.*

11. *Making sure every child feels safe, have a voice, and an adult will listen to them. Most of all, if they need, I am available to listen.*

12. *Helping the teachers make learning fun, engaging, relevant, and rigorous. Depending on the culture of your school, it could take some time. Remember that school is supposed to be engaging and we are preparing students to compete with students throughout the world. We have to be creative and cannot teach like we have in the past. Allow creativity and incorporate an abundance of writing.*

13. *Accepting responsibility for something I was not aware of and being humble about it. As a leader, if anything goes wrong, you are still responsible. It is important to make sure you know what is going on. Stay informed and make sure everyone knows your morals and values. Always have integrity, no matter the situation.*

14. *Being clear and concise with expectations or any request made.*

15. *Following policies, procedures, protocols, and holding people accountable.*

16. *Suspending a student and knowing that the suspension could have been prevented if certain protocols were followed and in place.*

17. Trying to get a staff member to recognize they were wrong and not make it seem like I was taking sides with a student/parent; Trying to get a student/parent to recognize they were wrong and not make it seem like I was taking sides with the staff member.

18. Working with PTA is essential. My PTA has helped me build relationships with people and businesses in the community. They have put on activities such as Harvest Festival, Craft Fair, Turkey Bingo, numerous dances, and so much more. As a result, the kids are able to see people and businesses that they know in the community at the school functions. Having a strong, supportive and active PTA is important.

19. Monitoring teacher lessons and perform observations. It is important to be visible, even if it is for five minutes in a classroom. The students and the teachers need to know that you are there and monitoring the teaching that is taking place. I am amazed by what I have seen in observations. For example, as a teacher, I hardly ever sat at my desk, and there are a number of teachers that do.

20. Building a relationship with businesses in the community and have the business leaders participate in school activities to expose the students to their local businesses.

21. Helping staff build a collaborative relationship with families to help students follow school policies and improve academically.

22. Keeping record of staff performances to determine if they are a good fit or not for the school environment. Having to make the decision to request a teacher be released from their position is one of the hardest decisions I have ever had to make. However, the greatest good of the children is most

important and running an effective organization is vital.

23. *Choosing trainings that are necessary and needed to help develop the staff.*

24. *Making sure that all staff (custodial, bus drivers, cafeteria workers, and all instructional assistance) were treated fairly and as a professional.*

25. *Getting up and going to work on days I do not want to go.*

26. *Managing the school budget wisely while ensuring the staff and students were able to have the needed materials and resources to teach and learn. Never writing a check or touching the money. Always keeping my hands off and away from any money.*

27. *Remaining professional, nonpartial, or non-vindictive after being disrespected, insulted and treated maliciously.*

28. *Showing gratitude and building up my staff with lunches, prizes, and treats from the social committee, vendors, and personal funds.*

29. *Not allowing the negatives, lies, or defamation to consume me.*

30. *Trying to balance personal and work is a continuous journey!*

This list includes some of my most important best practices in my position, but this does not include everything. Daily, there is something new to face. Every day presents its own challenges. It is important to stay prayed up and remember that a leader is not supposed to show when they are "shaken." A leader has to be emotionally balanced and stoic in many ways. You have to let go of the desire to be playful with everyone. A leader cannot allow friendships to cloud their mind or the atmosphere of professionalism. This can lead to people getting hurt and the culture will be impacted negatively. Therefore, remember to treat everyone respectfully, have boundaries, be professional, fair, and remember that everything you do impacts the culture of the organization/school.

During my journey to become a principal, the specific activities/programs that have assisted in my development are my education at Regent University and the two different assistant principal training programs that I participated in upon being selected for the Assistant Principal Pool. These programs gave me insight as to what I was going to have to do, the paperwork and the laws I had to follow as a principal. These programs also gave me more book knowledge and helped build my confidence about becoming an administrator.

Becoming an administrator was not an easy process in any way and my story is not everyone's story. I have met a couple of people who were practically given their position, and that is very different from what I had to deal with. However, I have had to accept that everyone has a different path and their path was not my path, and vice versa.

As I reflect on the different challenges I have had to face as a leader, the first is having to overcome racism. Despite what is said about racism, it is alive and real. On several interviews, I knew I had all of the qualifications, connected with the panel, and answered all of the questions appropriately, only to not be offered the position. When I requested feedback, I was told, "you were not a fit, but we do wish you the best." Not long after, I discovered that a candidate with fewer qualifications and of a particular race was given the position. Needless to say, I was devastated and frustrated. In the midst of my frustration, I turned to those that would encourage and help me push forward. This was not an easy process. To overcome racism, I have never given up on my dream of becoming an administrator, and I have been flexible and open to going wherever the good Lord would open a door for me. I also surrounded myself with people who would encourage me to not give up and continued to grow while I waited for a door to open. Now that I am an administrator, I have a clearer perspective. I remind myself that I am not the problem, but the problem is the people with lack of knowledge or willingness to accept diversity.

The second largest challenge I have faced is working with someone who actively tried to make me fail. In this scenario, I had to document everything, follow all policies and procedures, continue to be a professional, and remember that it was not about me and that I was not at fault. The way I was able to overcome this situation was not giving up, praying for guidance and strength daily, avoid being vindictive, remember that I was in the position to make a difference in the lives of children, and treat everyone fairly and respectfully. Overcoming conflicts with people who want you to fail is not easy. If you are ever in this experience, you will go through many emotions, question your abilities, and continuously wonder if there is or was anything you could have done differently. The answer is you can't control anyone but yourself. As you face your challenges, don't give up, pray for strength and guidance, and walk in integrity. Remember that, in the end, every day is a new day and you can overcome any challenges that come before you.

As you face each new day and you reflect, be sure you know why you want to become an administrator. Becoming an administrator should never be about the title or pay. The title "principal" is really overrated because of the amount of work and responsibility you will have compared to the pay. Remember, you are fully responsible for every single detail of everything that takes place in the school. Definitely delegate to try and balance some of the workload, but make sure you know what is going on. My advice would be to prepare yourself mentally, emotionally, and professionally before making that transition. No matter how ready you think you are, you will be challenged and made to question everything you thought you knew or learned. Surround yourself with people that will pray, support, encourage, and guide your steps. Keep your family, mentors, and God close because you will need all of them to keep you grounded and focused on why you decided to become an administrator or even went into the field of education.

As I close, I will add that I have learned in my role as principal that it is important to continue to grow by reading, learning about new strategies, seeking counsel from those that have been administrators, being flexible, never thinking you have arrived, being ethical, and staying in prayer. Although I have faced challenges, I am grateful because those challenges have helped me become who I am today. More than anything I love seeing the smile on the faces of the children and hearing, "Thank you" from parents and staff. Yes, there are days I wonder if there is something else, I should be doing—the challenges can be exhausting, but our work here is too important. Future leaders need to be developed. We are developing life-long learners. In the end, we must keep our heads up, learn something new every day, try not to take anything personal, and spread the love of learning. We can do this!

About Dr. Shirley P. Auguste

Dr. Shirley P. Auguste's *career began in 1991 as a teacher's assistant in Henrico County, VA while attending Virginia Commonwealth University for her undergraduate studies. In her 2nd year, she was placed as the Writing to Read Coordinator at the same school. It is during her years in Henrico County that she found her love of teaching and working with students in Title 1 schools. Since her humble beginnings as a teacher's assistant, she has been in education for over 25 years and taught a combined second and third grade, all grade levels from PreK to third grade, middle school Literature Circle, eighth grade Science, taught prep classes for GED/SAT/ACT, served as a team lead, before and after school tutoring coordinator, and served as an Assistant Principal. Dr. Auguste has served on numerous education boards such as School Advisory and the Association of Supervisory and Administration School Personnel. She has taught in a private school and in the public school systems of Virginia, Maryland, and Florida.*

After being in different leadership positions, she realized she could have a greater impact by being in administration. As a result, she pursued her administration degree and earned her Master's of Education in 2010 from Regent University. Her thesis was on "Closing the Achievement Gap between Black and White Males." Despite the challenges and struggles of being a Black Hispanic of Haitian descent, she pushed forward and refused to give up on any of her dreams. It is her belief that she can teach others how to do better by being a positive example.

Dr. Auguste went on to acquire her doctorate degree from Capella

University and wrote her first curriculum and defended "Developing 21st Century Leaders in K to 8th." She believes in helping teachers see beyond the student, so they can help their students believe they can accomplish more than what is in front of them. She wants to help students learn to love themselves and education so they can become life-long learners and overcome the negative stereotypes while learning how to make a positive difference.

Dr. Auguste loves to dance, travel, spend time with family and friends, and being adventurous. She credits her success as an educator and administrator to her mentors who have guided, consulted, and kept her encouraged. She is grateful for her children, family and close friends and all of their support and encouragement. She firmly believes that each person has played a role in her becoming the leader she is today and knows that every life she touches it is because of the knowledge and love that has been imparted in her.

D. JaMese M. Black

"Excellence is to do a common thing in an uncommon way."- Booker T. Washington

CHAPTER 3

"YOU KNOW YOU ARE A PRINCIPAL, RIGHT?"
MY JOURNEY TO PRINCIPALSHIP

By D. JaMese M. Black

I didn't want Education, Education wanted me.

"DaManda JaMese Morris" he called and I began my journey across the stage during my high school graduation. I remember thinking, I can not wait to get out of here and start my life! I was greeted and congratulated, even celebrated. " Are you going to become a teacher?" Many questioned. Your mom is such a great one. I smiled and replied, over and over,, "No Way!" I decided Education was NOT for me. I have lived this life. I watched my mother grade papers, work on the yearbook, worked games and even brought students home for days at a time. I also remember how her pay did not match the work she put in. I knew I wanted more.

I began college and found myself changing majors - Music, English even Nursing. None satisfied my soul. I dropped out. My parents were the sole providers for me. One day, there was a knock on my door with my dad standing on the other side. The conclusion of his visit left me with eleven dollars to my name and the need to find a job. I worked four jobs that summer, (two retail stores, a daycare center and a teacher's aide for high school summer school). Days passed, my routine became set and I was miserable. I slowly noticed the happiest of my days were from 12:00 - 4:00 pm. There was a teacher who noticed my excitement and instant connection with our students. She asked me to start creating a variety of ways to teach vocabulary to them. Each day, I had 45 minutes to make sure students learned new terms. This was AWESOME! The last day of summer school, the students showered me with cards, gifts and treats. Mrs. Jones turned to me and said, "You know you are a teacher." Have you considered becoming one?

There was a flyer posted for an Oratorical Contest hosted at a local college. I thought, well, I can talk! The award was a $1000 cash prize. I had bills. I stood to discuss the "Importance of understanding your decisions and how allowing your education to reach your goals."

I won.

The next day, I met Dr. Anderson, an Education professor, who provided me with the check and an offer to return to school. "Have you considered teaching?" he asked? " Your entire speech was a lesson. All you need is the activities to back up your standard. There are some students who need a person like you to educate them." I dropped my head. " I am not a teacher, I will not make money doing that." Dr. Anderson responded with a chuckle, " How is your bank account looking these days?" I graduated the following year with a degree in History and English with education certification.

There is joy in having a career that is your calling versus having a career just for money. That is the true definition of success.

Teaching My Way and in Many Ways

"Excellence is to do a common thing in an uncommon way."- Booker T. Washington

"Hey, JaMese." he smiled as he stood with his district during a teacher fair. Dr. George Reynolds walked around to provide a hug. "Well, you are a teacher," he stated. I nodded. " You are done looking. I will give you a call on Monday."

I began teaching social studies in a rural high school in North Carolina. I was one of three African American teachers with limited diverse students. This was one of the most rewarding yet difficult experiences. I learned how to menovur successfully among a community who does not support my existence as an African American or a woman. I begin living my belief of changing the world, one child at a time. I felt if I can change the way my students felt about me, and allow me to teach them, then my purpose as a teacher has been fulfilled. My schedule contained two repeater Civics classes and one regular Civics. Many students entered defeated. I begin building the individuals before building content. It became my goal for my students to feel their presence mattered before they could feel the content they learned mattered. I knew I mattered to them when they started to inform me of the date and location of the clan meetings. One honor I hold close to my heart.

A student who had not experienced success in Civics finally passed the End-of-Course Exam. His grandfather, the grand wizard of the area clan, was so proud of his grandson's success that he brought roses to give to this "Ms. Morris." "All I hear is this Ms. Morris. I want to meet this lady. He loves her and I think I do too." he shared with our schools' office manager. She notifies me to come down to receive my acknowledgement. When I walk into the office, our manager informs him who I am. He looks at me with complete shock as I stand there to hear what he wants to say. He turns to the *manager and says, "This short black girl is Ms. Morris?" She nodded. He laid the roses down and walked out of the office. Our manager informs me of his statement. I picked up the flowers and placed them in my classroom. I made a difference with my student.*

My teaching experience spans over four high schools, one middle school and one middle college. This includes rural, city and suburban. Three states: North Carolina, South Carolina, and Virginia. My philosophy of creating an environment of acceptance for all students- "You Matter"- maintained the same in every school. With this, still ensuring success required by the states and district expectations.

Everyday is an opportunity to bring sunlight to every student who walks into your classroom. Students must see your soul before your content.

Experience and Education, Oh My

A new middle college opened and introduced me to my forever mentor - Mrs. Charlotte Holmes. She asked me three questions during the interview and turned to me and said, "You are hired." I was one of the founding teachers. This was a small school and many teachers held several roles and titles. Throughout the year, I found myself becoming her second hand. If a student needed additional support (discipline, retrieval, tutoring, discipline plans, ect…), I found myself providing hands for the success of the student and school. There were many afternoons, we would just talk, plan and bounce ideas of innovative ways to reach our students. She constantly reminded us, she set the tone and high expectations for student success and she will model what is expected from us. "If I do it, you can too."

At the conclusion of our school year, we were having a reflection talk. This included deep and honest conversation about our success and failures (areas of focus) as a school. We were discussing my role this year and how it was hard for me to teach and complete other tasks. She took a deep breath, looked at me and said, " You know why?" I said, "Why?" She said, "You Know You are a Principal, Right? " I just looked at her.

I enrolled in the Educational Leadership program that summer.

Curriculum Facilitator- what is that?

"A job, need to take while you are working on this program," she said. This is a chance for you to spend time building teachers and providing them with assistance and instructional strategies to reach all students. This was the hardest and most important position I have ever held. I was forced to realize that there are different perspectives within the education realm for states, districts, schools and teachers. In order to be successful, I had to learn how to approach people and watch how others view me as a leader. As a curriculum facilitator (CF), this person is the "middle person" between the teachers and administration, it is key to stay consistent and state facts. This position helped me to maintain professionalism and look deeper into the true purpose of curriculum and standards. A successful CF, has the ability to motivate all teachers to celebrate their strengths and openly work to alter areas of weakness; while maintaining a positive open relationship of communication with administration to meet the school's goals. My role was critical for my growth due to the need to support teachers in the arts, career and technical along with content areas. I refer to this experience daily to help me maneuver as a principal. This position introduced me to a strong but graceful educational leader, Dr. Ester Coble. Under her leadership, she taught me how to speak with strength but yet remain graceful in the process. She would remind me it was not my job to uphold the stereotype of African American women but to redefine expectations. She employed me to carry myself so others would eagerly seek to hear what I have to offer. This was a moment of definition for me. I still strive to reach these goals everyday.

Walking a fine line can teach deep lessons of success.

API, Who Me?

Assistant Principal of Instruction is a position with two hats. My job was to ensure daily that I supported the mission and vision of the district and principal while maintaining high quality instruction and progression of growth and academic performance. I held this position under three principals who had completely different visions and processes/management styles. This experience taught me the importance of documentation and stating the facts and removing personal out of the equation. My focus during this time was to make sure our school shined by any means necessary, for my belief was and still is: If my work looks good, then my leadership will look good. This position also taught me the value of networking and connections. This is always something new to learn for success. The key was to stay humble and stay at a place of correction. My last year in this position, I believe it was time to push me into my own leadership. One evening after a long week, my principal called me into his office to share this statement: "The board has informed me that your work is outshining me as principal. I will not let you be a better principal than me, especially a woman." I remember sitting in my office, reliving every action, step I took, every decision I made, revisiting all my data and thinking this could not be true. I reviewed every document submitted that did not have my name on it but his and thinking this could not be true. I remember reviewing all the nights I stayed away from my family, working on different needs while others were gone home and thinking this could not be true. I was devastated.

Two weeks later, there was a call.

> *I don't have to be well-known, popular or even liked; as long as my students understand that I am fair and care- My job is done.*

Who Knew This Would Be So?

The newspaper read, JaMese Black named principal of my hometown high school.

Home.

This was a major step for me as more of a personal letter than professional. As mentioned earlier, my mother taught for fifty years in this district. One of her goals she did not reach was to become a Principal. She would always say, she chose to be a mom over progressing in her career. This was an opportunity for her to see me fulfill her dream. I was so fortunate to find myself surrounded by people who understood that I needed time to transition from assistant principal to Principal. I felt supported and was pushed to see their desire to see me succeed. My superintendent would have a "pep rally" with me around every three months to keep me motivated as I transitioned.

> *There is a reason why the chairs behind the principal's desk are larger than others. The weight is heavier to carry. The seat must hold both.*

Wait, We Are Not Accredited?

October 2014 (three months into my first principalship), I was invited to a meeting. I strolled in and greeted the other principals there. I noticed they were carrying a somber load and struggled to smile. I continued to chat until the meeting was called to order. I listened to my leadership discuss the celebrations of the schools represented, I even stuck my chest out while my school was discussed. Then they transitioned to the purpose of the meeting: Accreditation. I listened to them discuss their concerns and what they felt needed to be done to provide support to our schools. I heard them discuss the different levels of accreditation and how far or close we were to meeting the goal. I just sat there. I received my documents and data. I just sat there. At the conclusion of the meeting, we were given a pep talk and dismissed. I just sat there. As other principals left, I stood up and stopped the Assistant Superintendent and said, " Wait, we are not accredited?" She looked at me and said " No, you are not and we need you to fix it this year."

I drove back to my office in tears. What in the world did I walk into? Where do I start? It is October! How? Why? I immediately called my brother. He drove up and we prayed. "Renewed Minds" became my force. A community meeting was called where the latest information was shared. I stressed the need for them to think a different way, teach a different way, plan a different way. We must be different. We adapted a school-wide hashtag as a guiding force for all decisions. This was a daily battle of data dives, test mapping, interactive lessons, ect.. First semester exams are taken in December. We revamped schedules, changed classes and continued with our change process. Second semester exams are taken in May. We were all on pins and needles. Many were waiting to see if all the changes were relevant or was it a flop, as our scores were released, we began to celebrate. We were accredited.

Unexpected experiences creates your divine path in changing the lives of others

Are You Serious?

"Messie, I am not getting better. My time on this earth is short. Will you do me a favor?" she said. " Yes Momma, anything you want." " I want you to be here with me. I want you to step down and be with me until I leave." I stopped. "Mom are you serious?" She slowly nodded. I didn't have a backup plan, I just knew. My mother had given me all she could and never asked for anything in return. I owed her that. I called a meeting with my leadership team to share my plan to step down. " Are you Serious?" he asked. I explained. I owed her this. I sent an email to my staff for a call "Community Meeting" on April 1, 2017. I shared with them that I

will be stepping down for my mother. The shock on their faces. Many thought it was an April Fool's Joke. Many asked, "Are you serious?" So many other leaders informed me that it would be difficult as a woman leader to walk away from leadership and to return at a later time. Many would not believe your reason and will question your reality versus what the "norm" is. My last day as principal was on May 30, 2017. Mom passed July 3, 2017. " Mom, are you serious?"

My choices are always about children, except when it comes to my family.

Where I am supposed to be…

Interview, Interview, Interview… I listened to people celebrate my work and pass me over. Interview, Interview, Interview…. " I think you will outshine me as a principal." Interview, Interview, Interview… "Thank you for that explanation for leaving your thriving school. Now do you mind telling us the truth?" Interview, Interview, Interview… " Wow, we Googled you, you have a lot to offer. But, this position will be given to…" This happened for an entire year. I began questioning myself, my skills, my talents. I experienced broken promises and missed opportunities. I remember receiving the call for the next interview. I just didn't have it in me. I had three in one day. I remember making a bet on what the reason would be why I am not hired. I made my way. Three calls, three offers, my sacrifice had been acknowledged and rewarded.

Some may not understand it, but it is important to

Respect Your Journey

About D. JaMese M. Black

D. JaMese M. Black's *career in education began at Rockingham County High School, Wentworth, NC in 1998, where she was a social studies teacher. She served as a social studies teacher for seven years prior to becoming Curriculum Facilitator at Weaver Academy and Early/Middle College at Bennett in Greensboro, North Carolina, a position she held for four years. She was Assistant Principal of Instruction at Bartlett Yancey High School in Yanceyville, North Carolina from 2008-2009 and at Northeast Guilford High School in McLeansville, North Carolina from 2011-2014. She became principal of Magna Vista High School in Ridgeway, Virginia in 2014. She transformed the school to become accredited within one year. She led Magna Vista until 2017 upon her decision to step down to care for her mother. She returned to administration as Principal of East Montgomery High School in Biscoe, NC in 2018. She is the 2019-20 Principal of the Year for Montgomery County Schools. This, given after her first year in the district and turning around her school within the year to make growth.*

Black holds a Master's degree in Educational Leadership and a Bachelor of Arts degree in History and English from High Point University.

JaMese is the wife of Marquis Ron "Rico" Black and the mother of their twin boys: Ocir JaRon and Zyon JaRiq Black. She is the daughter of Rev. James and Sallie Morris-Redd; both have crossed into eternity. She is the youngest of three- Derrick JaSal Morris and Rev. DaRon JeSie Morris hold the title of her brothers.

Kirsten Clark

"Do what you feel in your heart to be right, for you'll be criticized anyway."
-Eleanor Roosevelt

CHAPTER 4

THE ROAD LESS TRAVELED

By Kirsten Clark

The plan was never for me to be a school principal, or even go to college for that matter. In high school I heard phrases like, "College isn't for everyone, Kirsten" and "It's too bad you're not smart like your brother". I allowed others to determine my life's path at that time. I didn't think much of it then, because no one in my family had gone to college, so it certainly wasn't an expectation.

After I graduated high school, I entered the workforce. I ended up working in a well-established law firm where I eventually became the office manager. I enjoyed my job and the attorneys I worked for, but something was missing. I wanted to accomplish something for me. I wanted to make a difference. I decided I wanted to go to school to be a teacher. I applied to Purdue University and did not get accepted, but I would not be deterred. I started taking night classes at our local Ivy Tech Community College, and after a year of core classes, I applied to Purdue again. This time I was accepted. I was twenty-three years old and had a full-time job, a car payment, and a place of my own. When I received my acceptance letter from

Purdue, everything changed. I moved back into my parents' home, commuted to campus, and could only work part-time. I left my job at the law office and started to work at a local warehouse that employed Purdue students. The transition was not an easy one. My mother even questioned if I felt I had made a mistake, but I knew in my heart that I hadn't. After a semester, I got my job back at the law office and worked around my class schedule. I took the dreaded 7:30 a.m. courses so that I could have my afternoons free for work. I put everything I had into getting my education. I made the Dean's List every semester and ended up graduating with distinction and cords. I gained confidence that I never had before. I earned my degree, and no one could take it from me. This is a topic I revisit on a regular basis with my students. Once you earn your education, it's yours. No one can take it from you. Others may be able to take your faith, your pride, your trust...but never your education.

My time at Purdue flew by, and in my last semester of coursework, I got married the week before final exams. I would not recommend planning a wedding in the middle of a college semester, by the way. I did my student teaching in the Fall of 2001 and returned to work at the law office once again upon completion. In the Fall of 2002, I was offered a teaching position at the same school where I completed my student teaching. I am loyal to a fault and didn't want to leave my bosses and co-workers, but I had worked so hard to earn my degree, and I wouldn't let it sit idle. I excitedly accepted the position and began my career in public education.

I spent 11 years in a high school social studies classroom. I taught World History, United States History, and Sociology. During that time I also coached cheerleading and dance team and was a co-sponsor for the National Honor Society. I had my first, and only, child while I was teaching, and unfortunately went through a painful divorce as well...both while I was in the process of earning a Master's Degree in Educational Technology from Indiana University Purdue University Indianapolis (IUPUI) during the evenings and on weekends. These life changes were incredibly difficult for me, and school soon became my second home. The colleagues I met over the years became family to me. I could depend on them to be there for me and my son, who has essentially been raised in a school, and pick me up when I stumbled. These are the friendships that have stood the test of time and will always be treasured.

I knew from the beginning of my teaching career that the school setting was where I truly belonged, but it wasn't until a new principal came along that I genuinely felt I had more to offer my students than what I was already giving. Dr. A. believed in me, and that helped me believe in myself. She taught me many invaluable lessons about being a leader. As a principal, she meant business, but she had a fair balance of compassion as well. She had high expectations for herself, and she held her staff to those same expectations. She was demanding, and many times this characteristic in women can be seen in a negative light, but she made it a positive as she challenged us to do better, to be better. I firmly believe that people, when challenged, will rise to the challenge. This is true for students and staff alike. Set the bar high, and most will strive to reach the bar. Set the bar low, and those are the results that you will get.

Dr. A was the first female principal I had ever encountered. My own elementary, junior high, and high school administrators were all male...not even a female assistant principal in my thirteen years. When I began teaching, our principal was male. I never thought much about the gender of an administrator until Dr. A came along. Dr. A became the principal in my school during a transitional period of my life. I was a newly single mother and struggling to find my way. She was somewhat of a no nonsense leader with high expectations for us all, but she also cared deeply about her staff and students. She allowed me to open up to her about my struggles, and she celebrated with me when my life started to turn around. When I hit the seven year teaching wall, she listened to my frustrations and wonderings about what I should do next in my career. Most importantly, she listened to hear me, not to respond and tell me how to proceed. So many of the things she said to me have stuck, and I will never forget the way she made me feel about myself as a mother, an educator, and a strong woman.

Dr. A showed up at my classroom door one afternoon and asked me to step outside. My mind was racing, wondering what I could have done, and my stomach instantly knotted up. She had found out that I was planning to remarry, and my future husband was also a teacher in the same school. She cried as she expressed to me how happy she was that we had found each other, not only for our own well-being, but for that of our respective children as well. My boss was truly joyful about my happiness, and that spoke volumes to me.

Five years later, when Dr. A announced that she was moving on in her career, I at first felt somewhat angry...angry that my role model and such a strong woman and leader who had brought our staff and students so far was leaving us, leaving me. I soon realized, however, that my feelings were selfish and that she was doing what was in her best interest, personally and professionally. How could I be angry with her for that? Before she left, she told me that I was a "woman of substance" and that I had much to offer. I will always hold those words close to my heart.

I reach out to Dr. A periodically to update her on my career and express my gratitude for the lessons I learned through her leadership. She is always supportive and encouraging, no matter the distance between us. As I listen to the clicks and cadence of my high heels when I travel down the terrazzo hallways of my school, I am often reminded of the petite, Italian fireball that she was. And if I can provide even a fraction of the guidance and leadership for someone that she did for me, I will consider myself successful.

In 2012, with much encouragement from my husband, I started taking courses toward my administrator's license at Indiana Wesleyan University. I was already working in the main office a few periods a day in a technology based position, while still teaching the remainder of the day. My time as an administrator came long before I had anticipated. Unexpectedly, I found myself serving as an interim assistant principal before I even finished my coursework. On one particular Tuesday in November of 2013, I was a teacher. On Wednesday, I was filling the position of an assistant principal. The transition was not as smooth as I would have liked. Going from being a colleague to an evaluator wasn't popular with everyone. Another challenge arose as the second AP position was vacated soon after I started. It was trial by fire, if you will.

I spent close to four years as an assistant principal in a school I loved. The job was hard. It was stressful. My duties included discipline, attendance, special education liaison, evaluating teachers, alternative school liaison, assisting the counseling department with standardized testing, SAT coordinator, ACT coordinator, etc. You can try to list all of the duties of an administrator, but it's never ending, and some cannot be classified with an official title.

I did miss being in the classroom with my students, but being an assistant principal allows you opportunities to build relationships with students that you may not have had as a teacher. Being a disciplinarian isn't a walk in the park, and I personally don't believe that it is a sustainable job for an extended period of time, but the flip side was being able to dig a little deeper with students to find the root cause of their behavior. Some of their stories were heartbreaking, and having that kind of knowledge about our students is a great burden to bear. Those are the students that you go to bed worrying about at night and make a point to follow up with the next day. Those are the students that need someone in their corner the most. Once they know they can trust and rely on you, they will be more apt to come to you when they need help, rather than acting out.

I never imagined that I would leave this school. It had become my second home over the 15 years that I was there. I met some of my greatest friends in that building. I was given a second chance at love in that building. I had gone through the best and worst times of my life in that building with those people. But then the principalship opened at my high school alma mater, which is a mere eight miles down the road and the district in which we live. I had never had a burning desire to take on the role as principal, but I soon changed my mind. This was my opportunity to lead the school I had attended. I had to take the leap.

My first day as principal was one day before the staff reported for school and two days before students. I think my adrenaline, and a tremendous administrative team and staff, got me through for months, maybe even the entire first year. I often say that "I didn't know what I didn't know" at that time. Once I figured out everything that I didn't know, the stress and anxiety kicked in. The principalship is a job that requires a great deal of behind the scenes work. In a small school such as ours, there isn't a central office filled with directors to take charge of all of the different programs associated with a public school, which means that the administrators take on the duties traditionally filled by those directors. The paperwork, deadlines, communications with the State, professional development workshops, etc. that are required for these programs take up a great deal of time, and that time has to come from somewhere. Unfortunately, it most often comes from time that would be better spent in classrooms.

One of the greatest challenges for me as a principal is the feeling that I do not spend enough time in classrooms. The best, and most important, part of my job is being in classrooms. After all, this is where the magic happens. In my second year as principal, I began a "No Office Day" initiative. In order to ensure that I get into classrooms, I am intentional about designating No Office Days. I schedule a day, communicate the day to teachers, and ask them to let me know if there is something happening in their classrooms on that day that they would like for me to observe. The invitations generally roll in, and I mark my calendar accordingly. I purchased a mobile cart to carry my laptop, radio, notebook, phone, etc. and roll it through the hallways as I make my way through the school. My entire day is spent with teachers and students, including lunch. No Office Days are not for formal observations/evaluations. This is a day just to observe. I have found that through No Office Days, the staff and students are more at ease with my presence in the classroom. The same is true for me, as I am more apt to participate in an activity that is occurring or ask questions during a lecture. I average around 20 classroom visits for every No Office Day. I am never more exhausted than on these days, but I am also never more inspired.

I oftentimes, as a teacher and assistant principal, thought about ways in which I could make more of a difference with our young ladies. I had gone through my own personal and professional struggles through the years, and I wanted to be able to show them that the issues they deal with are not unique to them, and in fact are issues that the adult females in their school went through as young ladies and are possibly still dealing with as an adult. I wanted to be able to provide them a safe space to be with other young ladies where there would be no expectations, no competition, and no judgment. I wanted to be able to provide them with the tools to find their voice, stand up for what they believe in, and to build each other up. I wanted to empower our young ladies and show them what is available to them and the different opportunities that lie ahead. When I became a principal, I saw these ideas come to fruition in what I like to call my passion project. I spoke with our Counseling Department and Media Specialist, and after several brainstorming sessions, we created the Fierce Female Series.

The Fierce Female Series was designed for our young ladies in grades 7-12 and their mothers (or other female figures in their lives). We hold evening events throughout the school year during which we have a female faculty member tell their story, an activity based on the theme of the evening, and a featured speaker from outside of the school. The faculty story is important because it allows our students to see that their teachers, counselors, and administrators are people too, with our own struggles and fears. I firmly believe that when they hear our stories, our young ladies feel a deeper connection with us. Through our featured speakers, our young ladies have been exposed to successful women in various professions, including a military veteran and entrepreneur, a local news station morning anchor, and our State Superintendent of Public Instruction. They have been told how these women have faced and overcome adversity in their journeys, how they handle failure, and the grace they have shown in their successes. They see all the possibilities that the world has to offer, many stating, "I never even knew that profession existed". The Fierce Female Series was designed for our students, but I have to be honest in saying that I have learned as much from it as they have, and it is a program in which I feel the most sense of pride as a principal.

I see my principalship as an incredible opportunity to reach students, to see issues from their perspective, and to make a difference in their lives. The same is true for faculty and staff. I have been given the chance to serve my community in a way that not many others ever will or can even begin to understand. This opportunity to lead is not something I take lightly. I consider myself to be a servant leader, and my desire is to give more than I get. I understand that when a student or staff member walks through the front door of the school in the morning, they are carrying baggage from outside. My hope for everyone is that for seven hours a day that baggage can be checked at the door, we can meet our students where they are, and we can provide what they need at that time...academically, emotionally, nutritionally, and physically. I may only be in my third year as a principal, but I believe that what I lack in experience, I make up for in heart. I am emotionally invested in my school, my staff, and my students, and I *take pride in my work with them all. I can only hope that that translates to them. This job is hard work, but more importantly, it is heart work.*

About Kirsten Clark

Kirsten Clark is a Jr.-Sr. High School Principal who works with approximately 550 students in grades 7-12 and a faculty and staff of 50 in a small, rural school in central Indiana. After spending eleven years teaching in a high school social studies classroom and four years as a high school assistant principal, Kirsten made the transition to principal at her high school alma mater and is now serving in her third year.

Kirsten is passionate about the importance of education for all students as well as the empowerment of young women. The Fierce Female Series was born from this passion and provides young ladies in her school the opportunity to hear the stories of successful women from the community and their perseverance in overcoming obstacles along the way.

Kirsten holds a Bachelor's Degree in Social Studies Education from Purdue University, a Master's Degree in Educational Technology from Indiana University Purdue University Indianapolis, and her Principal Licensure from Indiana Wesleyan University.

Kirsten is married to Troy Clark, a high school art teacher, has one son, Jack, two bonus daughters, Riley and Haley, and three grandchildren, Emberlynn, Kashtyn, and Kyzer.

Tiawana Giles

The greatest glory in living lies not in never failing but in rising every time we fall.
~Nelson Mandela

CHAPTER 5

FEARLESS LEADERSHIP

By Tiawana Giles

Past Principals, Ms. Burgess, Ms. Kihm, Ms. Johnson, Ms. Townes & Dr. Hooker, have had a tremendous impact on my leadership journey. They were critical in my development. I am a principal today because of them. Mrs. Burgess was one of the most compassionate people I ever met. She believed in everyone and it showed in how she interacted with everyone. Her love for people was evident in all that she did and represented. I loved her for how she treated everyone. She was fair and always believed in everyone. . Ms. Johnson was my first official mentor. She was the 2016 National Distinguished Principal in Virginia and I looked up to her. She showed me that all things are possible regardless of where you start and how high the deck may be stacked against you. . Your heart must be in this work and success will come. Ms. Kihm was very charismatic. She meant business and always had a smile on her face. Mrs. Kihm taught me how to be a professional, I am grateful to her for that. Mrs. Townes was truly my favorite principal. I respected her more than she will ever know. I often saw myself in her, how she interacted with people, her level of professionalism, her sense of humor and her knowledge in reference to how to navigate the principal ship. Under Mrs. Townes I learned how to be a principal. I am more than grateful for her leadership and guidance. Finally, my Principal Director, Ms. Quarles. She has such high expectations. Ms. Quarles always provided honest feedback that allowed me to develop as a leader. She truly impacted me and helped me to remain grounded in some of my most challenging moments. Her helping hand and belief in me, has allowed me to continue to grow and develop as an instructional leader. Hearing her tell me one day at a principal's meetings that she was proud of me, literally made my year. I lean on her words on the tough days. It's such a great feeling to have someone like Ms. Quarles on your team.

I started my career in education after serving five years active duty in the United States Army. I had a successful military career, but knew I wanted to teach. After earning my teaching license I started working as a fifth grade teacher in Maryland where I taught for four years. After leaving Maryland, I became a third grade teacher in Fairfax Virginia. I taught for eight years in Fairfax as an elementary and middle school teacher. I also served on several committees. I worked with amazing teachers in Fairfax. I loved my experience. It was tough to relocate to the Richmond area after getting married. I taught in Henrico, Chesterfield and became an assistant principal in Richmond in 2015. I served in that role for three years before being appointed Interim Principal and later Principal of G. W. Carver ES. Upon accepting the role to become the next instructional leader of Carver I had to make some tough decisions. The most important decision is hiring. Having the right people in the right place is critical to the overall success of a school. I look for the most committed teachers. Those teachers that understand their purpose and believe in the kids they serve. Carver Scholars need teachers who will go above and beyond to provide them a solid foundation for them.

Additionally, It was essential to secure outside resources and the right instructional support for students and staff. I would say to anyone, get the best people and work closely with them. Build your team and give them all the tools they need to be successful. Remain visible and supportive as you develop your team. Let them see you as a support for them and constantly check in with them. This I learned the hard way. As leaders it is critical we share the important role they play in our overall success as a school.

If teaching and learning does not happen at a high level the school will fail. It's important to recruit teachers and share your instructional vision with them early and frequent. As Principal Johnson shared with me this should be a part of all your correspondence with staff (emails, staff handbooks, weekly newsletters, and reiterated during staff meetings. Everyone in the school, impacts the school from the custodial staff to the principal. Having quality people is directly related to academic achievement and the school's overall level of success.

Systems and Structures

One of the managerial jobs of the principal is to outline the right systems and structures early. As a second year principal, I spent my first year and second putting systems and structures in place. This takes time to develop. Especially for new principals. It's so important to build relationships with our professional staff. This builds trust with your staff and allows your staff to get to know you. This translates to teachers going above and beyond to ensure the principals instructional vision is achieved.

I send out a weekly Carver Chronicle to our school community. There is a section for what's happening this week, a section for instruction, a section on culture and climate, celebrations (Birthdays, Peanut Award)In this part of the newsletter, I discuss expectations for the teachers, classroom, and academics. This outlines how we do things at G.W.. Carver ES or The Carver Way!

I have included a sample here

Challenges

Being a principal is challenging. We are the face of the community we serve. Rebranding and gaining the trust from the community was especially challenging for me when I was appointed in July 2018. The school was going through changes to include twenty-seven new staff members. I began hiring staff immediately and meeting with the staff that was there to hear their thoughts about the school. Through these one on one meetings with the staff I learned about the school and the staff as well. I still revisit my notes from the meetings.

As a principal, it's our job to provide positive leadership at all times. As I stated early, just as we want our teachers to build authentic relationships with our students and their families, principals must also do the same with staff. When building relationships with staff, principals have a little leverage because we supervise them. The community, on the other hand, takes time. In the twenty months I have served as the Proud Principal of Carver, I have seen some positive change occur with the support of our school community and our wonderful teaching staff. The community believes in the school, the district is proud of the school and our scholars can hold their heads high as future Carver graduates. Change takes time, however I am so proud of the work that has happened at Carver ES. One fundraising event netted the school more $107,000! We are forever grateful to the MAPS community and our school community for their support of Carver Nation. My goal as the principal and instructional leader is to have an educational platform that involves the community and continue to give them a voice and a school they are proud of.

My goal is to ensure G.W. Carver ES becomes one of the best elementary schools in the state of Virginia. We will continue to change the narrative for Carver. As we are Carver Nation_RPS. Being *"Carver Nation"* means involvement from the community, parents and teachers. Public Relations is about what others perceive. At Carver my goal with the help of our school community is to alter perceptions by being visible and doing the work that will make a positive difference in the lives of the children we serve. In the end it's all about perceptions. When someone says you don't have students' best interest in mind this is how they feel. I have to change that by staying positive and modeling the positive goals and outcomes we have made and will continue to make at Carver!

Advice for New School Leaders

Public Relations moves to the whole community and how you relate to everyone speaks how a principal leads. Instruction is about relationships. Our most rewarding experience is with people we connect with. We must keep this in the forefront when faced with a challenging situation. Whatever you do, it comes down to relationships. When people are angry and non-trusting, it comes with a level of discomfort. Principals are tested and challenged daily. We are put in a situation when you have to make tough decisions. Talking to parents and teachers while maintaining order in the school. Some decisions are difficult but this is what courageous leadership looks like. Superintendent Kamras asked us to **Lead with Love** in August of 2019. As challenges arose I learned more about the importance of Leading with Love and having positive intent, even if you are the only one. Principal should always be willing to lead by Caring and communicating with people to keep their respect, even if they don't agree. Leading with Love gives me the strength to return each day with a smile, because I know I grounded all decisions in what's best for kids. Being able to articulate a shared vision of what I wanted my school to become and how it fits into the community and explaining this to people of how we will get there was a part of my listening tour during my first 90 days and beyond. I still attend ALL my community events and take *an opportunity to share great things happening at Carver. The community is always welcome to visit and volunteer. This has been a game changer for our scholars in that the community has embraced Carver ES.*

As I am finishing my doctorate in education my research is focused on the under-representation of women superintendents in K-12 public education This book is aligned with keeping the spotlight on women who lead in education.

About Tiawana Giles

Tiawana Giles *comes with a wealth of experience in leadership and education. She has taught K-8th grade in Hawaii, Maryland and Virginia. She has served as teacher, assistant principal and principal serving over 5,000 students and 600 teachers in her over two decades in education. She is an avid reader and runner. Principal Giles holds a Bachelor of Science from Chaminade University in Hawaii, and Masters in Reading from Bowie State University of Maryland, and a Postgraduate Certificate from the University of Richmond. She will earn a Doctorate Degree from Walden University September 2020.*

Tiawana is a mother of two beautiful daughters, Jasmine Cunningham who serves her country in the U.S. Army, and Jada Cunningham who has followed her dreams of owning a Cheer Gym. She is the grandmother of Bobbi "Princess" Fulp and proud wife of Joe Giles. She resides in Virginia.

Principal Giles loves her school community where she has served as the proud principal since July 2018. You can contact Principal Giles via email tgiles2@rvaschools.net follow her on twitter @tiawanag and @GWCarver_RPS

Natasha McDonald

"Education is the most powerful weapon which you can use to change the world."
~Nelson Mandela

CHAPTER 6

GROWTH IS MANDATORY

By Natasha McDonald

Have you ever been around someone so inspiring that it fills your cup just to be in their presence? Dr. A. Tracie Brown is that person for me, and until she is gifted with this book, she will not know the magnitude of her impact on my school leadership. Dr. Brown is an Assistant Superintendent of School Leadership in a neighboring school district and the founder of a non-profit organization called Future School Leaders Network (FSLN).

I met Dr. Brown four years ago at a very critical time in my career when I had recently moved to a new city and school district. This move proved to be very difficult for me because in my previous school district, I was established and had fostered many meaningful relationships. I always joke and say "that district raised me," as the years spent there were some of the most difficult, yet rewarding, years. That period of my career can easily be described as my education leadership foundation.

While my new district was very welcoming, many of my days were spent feeling like the new kid on the block and I was very nervous about the work it would take to establish new relationships and credibility. I was also accustomed to being exposed to stellar professional development for campus leaders and felt lost when I sought out the same in my new home to find it was not the norm. The void of all of the things aforementioned created serious doubt and I started to seriously question my place in education, leadership in particular.

One day, while scrolling through Facebook, I saw a previous colleague's post about FSLN and its impact on her career and it caught my attention. I found myself in a rabbit hole researching about the program and decided to apply for the second cohort. Upon being invited, I found out that FSLN would be a big time commitment, as it meant I would spend one Saturday a month in class at Southern Methodist University (SMU) from 9-12 am, and that I would be required to do homework and outside of class reading, and all of this would be offered to me for *FREE!* When I told one of my colleagues at the time about the opportunity, he laughed at me and said "Who in the world would want to do that and not get paid or get college credits for it?" We bantered back and forth, but at my core, I knew I was hungry and that meant sacrifices must be made to ensure I continued to grow.

At my first meeting, I realized very quickly what a blessing this organization would be to my soul, and that I had "found my people." Dr. Brown had selected over 20 educators from around the metroplex to share in the learning and to be a part of cohort two. She set ground rules about FSLN and gave us her "why" for being intentional about mentoring school leaders. Our cohort gelled quickly and became known as "team too much," as we had found a safe space where it was acceptable and to be over the top about our craft and celebrated. Dr. Brown guided us through many learning experiences and through a book study of a book called "What got you here, won't get you there" by Marshall Goldsmith. She led us through exercises to help us identify our core values and created a space that allowed us to be transparent about our personal constraints, while holding us accountable to finding ways to recognize them in ourselves and manage them.

Dr. Brown brought in area Human Resource Directors and hiring managers to talk us through what leadership looks like to them and the types of things they are looking for, helped us with our resumes and even conducted 1:1 mock interviews to help prepare us for our next opportunity when the time came. She reminded us frequently that each day, we represent our own brand and as well as hers and that we are also interviewing for our next position. She called out greatness in each of her mentees and gave so much of herself, all while leading a school district and being in school for her doctorate degree and she never charged us a single penny.

With FSLN, I developed relationships that will transcend moves from a school district or city. Although our Saturday class sessions are complete, we continue to collaborate and talk through challenges without the fear of retaliation or discussions being shared beyond the intended audience. Many of us, including myself, who have been so blessed by this organization were invited to stay with FSLN as Ambassadors because the program has grown so large. The Ambassadors are available to help Dr. Brown as needed to help continue her leadership vision to include more leaders. One of her many quotes that sticks with me is "Every time you move up a level, be sure to reach out to an aspiring leader. After all, someone did just that for you." -ATB

She is a very passionate leader who challenges me to be my best self and fills my leadership cup. If you don't have a mentor, or someone who helps you to identify and tackle your personal constraints, yet celebrates you for your wins, I highly suggest that you find one!

As a campus principal, I make decisions for over 1000 people daily. In the day and age of the school shootings and child molestation and abductions, my number one priority is safety for everyone.

Administrators must work to ensure we have systems in place to protect everyone and that everyone makes it home safe to the people they love the most. That is a big burden to carry, one that I honestly never signed up for, but inherited. We have a school resource officer to ensure our safety and we practice drills to make sure we are prepared in the event of disaster. While I loathe the fact that we have to do this work, I am a firm believer that learning cannot take place when basic needs are not met.

The second most important decisions I make are ensuring high levels of learning for all students. I have to provide clarity for all expectations and work to ensure we are all working towards the same mission, vision, values and goals. This includes global decision making that is sometimes unpopular. When possible, I practice shared decision making and have different leadership teams to research and guide the work that we do. It is up to me to articulate and inspect the things that we hold tight vs. loose. One of the most important things that is held tight on our campus is collaborative planning. This valuable practice exposes all our kids to the best of our staff. Ideas are shared, practiced and refined through this process. It also exposes our campus needs to ensure that as the campus principal, I am selecting the right professional development opportunities for my staff.

It is important to ensure that all staff believes that all students can learn and that they work to instill the growth mindset in the students. As a leader, I must ensure a positive campus culture and model being a lead learner. Principals are responsible for hiring and retaining the staff members that embody the growth mindset, as you cannot give what you do not have! I recently heard someone say that a campus takes on the personality of its principal, and I never understood that until I recently got the opportunity to sit in the chair.

With every decision I make, I think of the global impact of the decision on my entire campus. Wise leaders are very intuitive, and they quickly learn when to persist and when to abort a mission. I lead fearlessly, and with love. There are times that I must have crucial conversations, make unpopular decisions or hold people accountable, and while it is uncomfortable, it is my charge. If I am unwilling to confront issues that interfere with our mission, vision, values and goals, I am unfit to lead.

The best professional development activities and programs for educational leadership are the ones that transcend beyond the school house and make you a better person. To date, exposure to the Flippen Leadership Group, True Colors, Crucial Conversations and Doctor Adolph Brown, all have had a considerable impact on my life and leadership, as each of them consist of transferable skills that are applicable in both my personal and professional life.

The Flippen leadership group has many components, but I will take the time to share two of the key ones here. Capturing Kids' Hearts, also referred to as CKH, is a systematic way of building relationships. In schools, I have personally witnessed the fruit of the laborious task of being intentional about relational capacity and the impact on student achievement. With CHK, the adults are trained to establish norms in an unconventional way that gives everyone involved "voice." The norms then become the set of agreed upon behaviors and the organization becomes more self managing, as everyone knows what is expected of them. There are systems in place within CKH that help to ensure it is implemented with fidelity and integrity. People are taught non verbal hand signals to "check" peers who are not adhering to the social contract prior to being addressed by someone in an authoritative position. There are also raters and affirmers who serve to help keep us accountable to visit what we value. The use of sharing "good things" allows for celebrations and connections to be made within high performing groups. In the classroom setting, there are also four questions that help students to reflect and deviate from off task behaviors, which yields more time on task.

Flippen Blueprint leadership training has a great impact on intentional leadership. Prior to the training, you are asked to get the email addresses of people who you interact with on a frequent basis that can speak to your leadership and interactions. You are also expected to answer the same series of questions about yourself, so you can see how close your perception is aligned to the perception of others. In the interactive training, you are led to discover your personal constraints and are taught ways to address them, daily. You are taught that an organization cannot rise above the constraints of its leader, as the organization with the least amount of constraints wins. As a leader, you work with a coach to develop a traction plan to support your growth and an accountability partner to ensure that you don't get "too busy" to take the time to address your constraints as your leadership will definitely have an impact on student achievement, good or bad..

True Colors is a model of personality identification that is easy to understand, remember and apply. There are four colors: orange, gold, green and blue that are used to describe personality traits. True Colors distills the elaborate concepts of personality theory into a user-friendly, practical tool used to foster healthy productive relationships. True colors served as a HUGE asset to a previous campus. We learned about each color and what it represented as well as how to interact and how not to interact to get the most productivity prior to being given the quiz that revealed our own colors. As a campus, we decided to put our colors on stickers and affix them to our badges and also displayed them outside the doors of our classroom to represent our colors. The colors are not used for an "excuse" and a "that's just how I am" on our campus. It is used to show us how we need to communicate with the person that we are engaging with and it drastically improved the climate and culture of our school!

As leaders, we must get comfortable having difficult conversations. Crucial Conversations is a professional development course that teaches skills for creating alignment and agreement by fostering open dialogue around high-stakes, emotional, or risky topics—at all levels of any organization. You are taught how to frame your conversation and how to speak and be heard during times of difficulty. Crucial conversations help leaders make high-quality decisions, and the training gives you the tools to assist with following through to foster accountability and greatness. The training was phenomenal! It was interactive and practice opportunities were built in so that you could get immediate feedback so that you could get better at having them. After the training, I went and had two, much needed critical conversations and they both went extremely well. I even got a card saying "thank you!" This training not only helps with work, it helps with your entire communication. I have been able to recognize triggers in myself and have become a much better communication with everyone that I encounter. To date, I cannot count the amount of crucial conversations that I've had, but I can say that I consider this to be a strength, as many people have complimented my way with words and the skillful way that I address conflict.

Doctor Adolph Brown, affectionately referred to as Doc Brown, was a keynote speaker at a district convocation meeting where the entire district came together to kick off a new school year. He was a master at all things we hope teachers to be, especially when it came to classroom management. He was able to model inclusive practices in a colosseum of thousands of people. He walked us through ensuring that in our daily charge, all really does mean all with the expectation for our students learning at high levels and even used a wheelbarrow as a visual. The part that stuck with me the most was his intentionality of teaching everyone how to recognize balcony vs. basement people in our lives. He described a basement person as someone who always finds fault in things and who is ready to moan, groan and complain about all of the things that aren't going right. They are not known for having any solutions to problems, but are nearly professionals at pointing them out. He also challenged us to determine which we wanted to be and to acknowledge where we currently were, check our own biases and develop a plan.

The biggest challenge that I have faced as a school leader thus far is inherent distrust of the school personnel. There are many speculations as to why distrust exists, and to be honest, I personally think the sad state of our country's race relations is a huge contributing factor. As an African American woman who lives and leads in a predominantly white and Asian community, my experience has been reportedly different than many of my colleagues. To give you a glimpse into our diversity, I have listed my current district and campus demographics in the chart below.

Demographic Breakdown	Campus	District
White	36%	41%
Asian	28%	29%
Hispanic	11%	14%
African American	18%	11%
Two or more races	5%	4%
American Indian/Alaskan	1%	1%
Hawaiian/Pacific Islander	0%	0%

I've worked on campuses where teachers expressed dreading communication with parents due to the fear of being attacked. In certain instances, teachers refused to meet alone with parents and requested that either their entire team accompany them or that one of the administrators be present during communication. The request seemed a bit strange to me, but after attending a few contentious parent meetings, I quickly understood their fears. I also realized that they had not been properly trained on what to do when a meeting took a negative turn and the adults became verbally belligerent, abusive or attempted racial attacks on staff members. Over the years, I have spent a large chunk of time training teachers on how to deescalate and knowing when to call for help in the event of parents becoming verbally abusive or attempting to intimidate. Throughout my career, I've had to intervene in situations where parents attempted to have students removed from a class because of a teacher's religion, and cited the reason for the request as a language barrier. The truth was, there was no language barrier, we found that some people were not comfortable with staff members who wore hijabs. Of course, any invalid requests were not honored. I've been in situations where administrators had to ask parents to cease all written communication with teachers due to aggression towards the teachers and have also had to ask parents not to put their fingers in the faces of school employees in an attempt to intimidate. A down side to campus administration is the increased level of safety concern during times of conflict. I've been verbally accosted, been the recipient of harassing phone calls and I have been threatened a few times. Of course, we don't sign up for education for this dark side of the job. If we had things our way, we would love the presumption of positive intent and to collaborate in an effort to produce the best future leaders ever, but the harsh reality is that we do find ourselves in very challenging situations that require a very specific skill set to be successful as a leader.

When I was an Assistant Principal, I noticed that we experienced extreme behaviors that could be curtailed with a home/school partnership. I spent the majority of my days dealing with discipline. When I called home, because yes, I am old school, and still believe in the power of communication, I would get a resounding, why didn't anyone call me to tell me that my child did this or that before it got to this level. Sometimes, I would feel compelled to share some of the horror stories that happened when a phone call was made in a very generalized way, and other times, I would just apologize and tell them that I would have the staff member make the phone call to give clarity on the incident. As time went by and as I had the opportunity to build relationships with the students and parents, I realized that most of the negativity came from a place of distrust that had little do with the staff at the school, but it was more so stemming from things that were happening in society, in the news or with previous school districts/campuses, or even stemmed from the parents experiences as students.

I recently heard a colleague from FSLN say that you have to "Maslow before you Bloom," and this statement resonated with me as it described my current reality. I did not get to spend the amount of time that I needed to spend on instructional leadership that year because I had to spend time ensuring that the needs of the students and teachers were met. When my previous principal announced her retirement, and I spent time working on the work, I created a true 30, 60, 90 day and beyond plan that I felt would assess the root cause of the functions of the behaviors we were seeing. Through conversations, surveys and observations, it was revealed that part of the distrust was lurking because our staff demographics did not mirror our campus demographics.

Teacher Demographics	2018-2019	2019-2020
White	84%	75%
Asian	3%	4%
Hispanic	4%	7%
African American	7%	11%
American Indian	1%	3%

The more time I spent on the campus during my transition phase into campus principal, the desire to bridge the gap became stronger. In my mind, the only way to do so was through communication, education and tolerance of others. I have always found it easy to connect with almost anyone, and decided I would not back down from a challenge, as I often ask myself on difficult days "If not me, then who?"

Since then, we have worked through the following

- o *Porch visits- Our staff volunteered to give up an evening of their summer vacation to visit the homes of our incoming 6th graders. This was a tradition that many other schools in my district had done, but it was new to the families in our community. It was a ton of work on the front end coordinating the visits and preparing the gifts that we gave them, but it was very worth it. We were welcomed into the homes of our incoming students and we celebrated the partnerships through posting pictures of our visits on social media. That is definitely a tradition that we plan to continue as it was worth every single hour that was sacrificed.*

- *PBIS- Our staff went into year two of the implementation phase of PBIS, positive behavior intervention systems where we explicitly teach the behaviors that we expect to see and reward and focus on the people who are doing what is expected of them. We even launched a monthly school store where students can earn school currency and they are able to purchase items with their school money. The PTA partnered with us to donate enough items to sustain us through our entire first semester of school and a temple across the street, funded the rest. They made it happen for our students and it has been a huge success. The teachers and the students want to add the currency system to the classrooms and not just use it in the common areas.*

- *CKH- We helped our district to see the unique needs of our campus and they assisted us in finding funding to have my entire staff trained in Capturing Kids' Hearts and we are in year one of implementation. It has been a pleasure to see the systems working to curtail inappropriate behaviors and to have classes be more self managing. It has also been great to help teachers build relationships by having a uniformed way to address concerns ie. the four questions.*

- *Advisory interest groups- We believe that all students should have a mentor and be connected to someone on campus outside of their core classes. Each student selected an Advisory/Interest group based on their interest and teachers did the same, and they were paired by interest instead of grade level/skill. This has had pro's and con's so we are going to reexamine the effectiveness at the end of the school year by conducting a survey for the students and the staff to determine if this is a practice that we want to keep or if it is something that we need to rethink.*

- *Establishment of a Male mentoring program- The Xi Tau Lambda chapter of Alpha Phi Alpha Fraternity, Incorporated partnered with our school because our profession is dominated by females on the middle school level, with 80% of the professional staff being women. We were experiencing the most discipline problems from our male students, so we reached out to the fraternity to get a positive male presence around the campus and they showed up, did AMAZING things, and have had such a powerful impact on our male students. I'd like to give a personal shout out and say, thank you! Thank you for your selfless service. Thank you for your mentorship. Thank you for your Saturday morning sacrifices and more than anything, thank you for answering the call for our young men! The relationships that you have established and the experiences that you continue to afford them are priceless.*

These are just a few of the things that we have implemented to begin to build the bridge and tear down the walls of distrust. We have a long way to go, but I do see light at the end of the tunnel as we roll up our sleeves and do the most noble job ever, educating our replacements!

In 2017, I co-authored *Next In Line to Lead: The Voice of the Assistant Principal, Volume 1* and I shared the following leadership advice:

1. Keep a level head.

2. Don't make emotional decisions.

3. A decision does not necessarily have to be made today, but rather allow myself think-time.

4. Everyone deserves due process.

5. Sometimes the teacher really does make a bad choice, investigate and help to resolve conflict in a timely fashion.

6. Apologize on behalf of the organization when necessary.

7. Don't take things personally when people are angry, 9 out of 10 times, you are not the target.

8. Be clear with your expectations and ensure your staff knows what is tight and what is loose.

9. Visit what you value.

10. Presume positive intent.

11. Document, Document, Document!!!

12. You must first be accountable before holding someone else accountable...as a leader, people watch and will do as you do, not as you say.

13. Servant leadership takes you far.

14. "People don't care how much you know until they know how much you care" ~Flippen Leadership.

15. The golden rule is golden. Treat students, staff, community members, parents and all stakeholders how you want you or your family to be treated.

All of these things still hold true. As I've transitioned into a different leadership role, I'd like to add a few additional nuggets:

16. *What you feed grows, what you starve dies.*

17. *Clarity precedes competence!!!*

18. *Protect your peace.*

19. *Be present when it counts most*

    a. *Schedule "You time" even if it means getting a hotel room alone for the weekend.*

    b. *Be active and present during family time. You should not give to others what you are unwilling to give to those who love you the most.*

    c. *Be present at work and give 100% of the time you have while there to build relationships and attend to necessary issues while you are there.*

20. *Secure your mask before attempting to help someone secure theirs.*

21. *Find your Balance. It may not be pretty. It will require sacrifices. It is very important to avoid burnout.*

22. *Knowledge bears responsibility.*

23. *Integrity is what you do when you THINK no one is watching. Trust me, they are watching.*

Thirst for knowledge must transcend beyond what your school, campus and district are doing. Just as we expect doctors to be cutting edge and continue to learn and find ways to improve, we must be committed to do the same. As the campus principal, I work hard to be a lead learner. I empower my staff to make mistakes and grow from them, and in turn, I model the same mindset and ask for grace when I fall. I am as transparent as I can be with my struggles and I work very hard to create a culture where we celebrate more of what we want to see. One of the mottos I live by is, you don't have to be bad to work at being better. As I reflect on our practices, I live in a constant state of questioning if we are doing what is best for kids and preparing them for the jobs that they will create, not the ones that are currently available.

I reflect, I listen and solicit feedback. Feedback is food for my soul and as I tell my staff, please don't rob me of a growth opportunity from failing to give me feedback. I am intentional about soliciting feedback from my students, staff and community, and actually use the data to find relevant professional development sessions. I am very competitive and want to be the very best, so I am hungry to continue to perfect my craft. My latest Flippen Blueprint analysis revealed that I am very high on intensity. While this sounds great, it can be of detriment, as I have so intentionally slowed down and forced myself to understand that my pacing can stress others out, and that sometimes, less is more. When I am in that situation, I choose to do the learning to feed my own spirit, but I am selective about who I take along with me for the journey, as it might just be time to plant seeds and reap the harvest at a later date.

I am a member of TASSP (Texas Association of Secondary Principals) and I attend their yearly conferences and find written publications to challenge me. When I find something that speaks to me or a need on my campus, I share it. In fact, I subscribe to Marshall's Memo, an education publication that provides short articles to peak your interest and gives me nuggets of information to keep me up to date with what's going in the field of education within and outside of my world.

As mentioned earlier, I am also an ambassador for Future School Leaders Network, a non-profit organization. I started with the organization as a participant, and I did not want to depart from the learning experiences, comradery and relationships developed with *my peers in neighboring districts in our metroplex. We discuss current trends and we also spend time reconnecting with our why each year. As comedian Michael Jr. says, ``When you know your why, your what has more impact because you are walking in and toward your purpose."*

I am a firm believer in playing to one's strengths. While I do not have one specific "go to" for leadership, I am thankful to have a plethora of well-respected individuals that I lean on to seek council and bounce ideas back and forth depending on the need as educational leadership is multifaceted. I am very fortunate to have worked alongside many phenomenal leaders and instead of leaning too heavily on one person, I've intentionally formed my tribe of advisors based on areas that I see as their strengths.

Letycia Fowler, *my previous campus principal, is my deep analytical thinking partner who challenges me to think beyond what is in front of me. She challenges me to see the "gray" and not just think in the black and white that comes naturally for me.*

Terri Gladden, *my previous campus principal, is a culture guru and an all around fun person to be around. She helps guide me in picking my battles, and understanding that being "team too much," is quite alright. She takes the time to continue to mentor me, and has been a HUGE asset in this transition space I've found myself in stepping into the role of a campus principal.*

Dr. Alicia Maphies, *my previous principal and* Clint Cypert, Matthew Sears, David Alexander and Officer Avery Jones, *my previous colleagues are a team of solid leaders, whose work speaks for itself. They are truly a well-oiled machine where everyone is competent and able to step in and assist one another to ensure the success of the entire team. When I need to understand the workings of my current district, and how to navigate they are definitely the leaders I turn to.*

Lisa Molinar, *my previous supervisor and Director of State, National & Local Assessments is my testing guru friend. Texas is it's own country when it comes to state accountability and testing. I am so thankful that I can pick up the phone at any hour and she will still take the call and give me good testing advice.*

Tina Moore, *a previous colleague and now the Director of Advanced Academics is my fun and wise beyond her years friend. She answers when I call and gives me sound advice. She definitely is a beautiful soul who is gifted and talented, and I have a high level of respect for her council. She reminds me of my purpose when we interact, and for our time spent, I am so thankful!*

Dr. Markeba Warfield, *a previous colleague, sorority sister and now a campus principal, is my tell it like it is friend. She has been a principal for a couple years longer than me, and I am able to call her when I need someone to shoot it to me straight about decisions that need to be made. Although her schedule is just as hectic as mine, she lets me vent and then pulls me back up to the balcony with her! I admire her tenacity as she was able to finish her doctoral program while being a good wife, mommy and new principal.*

Maura Ayers, *a previous colleague, a previous principal, and most of all, a friend, is my spirit animal as a leader. It is eerie how our 2 year old daughters who are now 14 introduced us to one another and how we became great friends. I can call and bounce the craziest ideas off of her without the fear of judgement.*

Lakeiah Chetham, *a friend from FSLN's cohort #2, my sorority sister, a previous principal, and the creator of Edu-Dots, a non-profit organization created to assist with professional development for new teachers. She was a Godsend who came into my life at just the right time. She is so intentional about building relationships. She calls to check on me as she has walked a mile in my shoes as a campus principal and she prays for me through difficult storms. I am so thankful for our friendship.*

Mitzi Garner, Donnie Wiseman, Robin Scott, Anita Robinson and Chakosha Powell, *are all Middle School campus Principals in my current district. Our entire Middle School group is AMAZING, but these five go above and beyond to ensure that I am successful. I can call either one of them at any time for sound advice, and when I ask questions, they are always there to respond quickly and with great resources. The job of campus principal can be a lonely job, but not with this group of leaders. They are selfless and have embraced the all means all mentality, as they are willing to share with me more resources than I can stand to digest. There is no busy like new principal busy, and these five have been food for the soul!*

Ronnie Elmore, *my current Human Resources Director, is amazing!!! He works hard to keep me in compliance and is always just a phone call away! I am so thankful that we get to work together in this capacity. He has spent countless hours on the phone with me talking me through difficult situations and giving me sound advice.*

Phil Evans, *a Managing director and my current supervisor. He trusts my leadership as a new campus principal and is super supportive. He listens with intent, and asks intentional questions to help me think through problems that I present to him. He always has a "global"/end in mind focus and he connects me with the right people to help me when I am in need. I can't begin to share how thankful I am for him.*

My secretary, administrative team, instructional coaches, building leadership team, and the entire staff for the 2019-2020 school year, thank you from the bottom of my heart for embracing 2.0 with me and allowing grace during this year of transition. Our growth this year has truly been reciprocal and I could not think of a better group of people to start this journey with!

While my educational leadership tribe is AMAZING, I would be remiss not to mention my family as they are where I garnish my true strength.

Erica and Ella Brown, *my two older sisters, are the very reason I am as strong as I am today. I watched them make mistakes and they challenged me to learn from them and they always build me up. Those two will fight someone about me, and were intentional about making sure I was tough, confident, and ready for the world. I learned my first lesson of leadership watching them do all the 1st so that I could come behind them (due to the age gap) and do them differently, or at least, my way.*

Joyce and Richard McDonald, *my mother and father in law, took me in and have treated me just like I am their blood daughter from day one. They celebrate me and they challenge me to be courageous and to hold on to my core values.*

Sheri Herod, *my aunt, who is also one of my closest advisors and confidants. She drops whatever she is doing to take part in my shenanigans! She "gets" me and she engages me in my gazillion work conversations that I must get out before I get home, and she actually remembers and gives me sound advice. She is a very active part of our lives and she sacrifices so much for all of us.*

Ella and Chester Herod *(late), my mother and father, I believe true leadership starts at home. I got my out of the box creativity and kind heart from my mother and my work ethic and tenacity from my dad. I could go on and on about these two, but the sacrifices made for me mean the world. I just hope that I've made them proud with my leadership in my personal and professional roles.*

Amari and Addisyn, *my sweet daughters, are my true leadership gurus. They give me feedback on my ideas on what works for kids in school as they are currently in the trenches. They endure the long work hours of being an administrator's kid and attend all sporting events, concerts, and plays that I work without a single complaint. They do homework in the car and can often be found sleeping in my office or in a teacher's classroom late into the evening. Those two are the REAL MVPS!*

"Mr. Mac" Richard McDonald, *my husband, a small business owner, who is my biggest supporter and cheerleader outside of our children. He challenges me daily to avoid the pitfalls of comparison as he knows that I am a "recovering" perfectionist. He is a guru at relationship building and his heart for teaching kids how to think and not what to think drew me closer to him when we first met. He loves me at my worst and helps to uncloud my vision when I spend time comparing my bloopers to other's highlights. He is intuitive and encourages me to take time to spend time with myself and reminds me to actually be a little bit more selfish with my time. With him, I have learned to give 100% of the 50% of my day that is spent at school to school and 100% of the 40% of my day that is spent at home to home and to be intentional about carving time out for myself, the one person who is often neglected by me!*

I've never been the kind to want "yes people" in my circle, so my intentional leadership tribe consists of people that stretch me, question me and challenge me to be my best self. Each serves a different role in my life and I am a better leader because of each one of them. It is my hope that I am able to reciprocate the love and support of those who guide me. Each person mentioned has a unique niche or area of strength, but we all share in one common goal, and that is working collaboratively to ensure high levels of learning for all students, our future decision makers.

About Natasha McDonald

Natasha McDonald has been employed as a Texas Public Educator for a little over 15 years under the leadership of several phenomenal individuals. She has had the opportunity to lead as a Classroom Teacher, a Literacy Strategist, a High School Testing Coordinator, an Assistant Principal, and an Academic Dean of Instruction. She currently serves as a Campus Principal. A former Principal spent time mentoring her and ultimately inspired her to become an administrator. She is thankful that she has had the opportunity to serve in multiple roles and obtain a wealth of knowledge as each of the roles have prepared her for this moment in her leadership.

She has a passion for helping others see the best in themselves, and is very intentional about relational capacity. She absolutely loves children and understands that we must invest in them as they hold the key to our future. She juggles the roles of wife, mother, mentor, and educator while simultaneously leading an AMAZING middle school with a little less than 1000 students. She finds pleasure in learning new ways to impact student achievement, and challenges herself to address her own personal constraints daily. She is unapologetic about leading fearlessly and works to positively impact the lives of the people she serves.

She has completely embraced the growth mindset and practice being a lead learner on her campus. She is comfortable modeling the art of failing forward. When she does, she dusts herself off, adjusts her crown, and seeks ways to improve. A very wise principal once told her "You don't have to be bad to work at being better." She is so very thankful that she "gets" to lead in this capacity and is very humbled by the charge. The ability to obtain knowledge is a remarkable gift, and she puts her heart and soul into learning new things and sharing them with others.

Lydia Ryan

"Focus on the best in others and they will see the best in you" - *Lydia Ryan*

CHAPTER 7

"TRANSFORMING SCHOOL CULTURE: TOXIC, TO TOLERABLE, TO TEAMWORK"

By Lydia Ryan

I asked Ms. Green to meet with me. A few days prior I had observed her classroom and wanted to discuss some feedback regarding her classroom culture. She responded that she would meet me and would be bringing a colleague with her. This surprised me, though perhaps it should not have as the staff had recently established a new policy that all faculty members were allowed, and encouraged, to bring along a peer to any conversations requested with administrative team members. Ms. Green, therefore, brought one of our most veteran and vocal staff members with her to our scheduled feedback conversation. We will call her Ms. Cook.

Ms. Green and Ms. Cook sat and faced me in my assistant principal's office. After pleasant greetings, I launched the conversation by restating what I heard Ms. Green say to a special education student during class. It was a comment that sounded sarcastic in nature and one that the student had reported to me in confidence had made him feel belittled. However, Ms. Cook quickly interrupted me by instructing Ms. Green not to reply. "Ms. Green, end this conversation immediately and do not engage in conversations about this feedback until your union representative is present." This was not how I envisioned the conversation starting, which was a conversation that had not started at all. As calmly as I could I asked why Ms. Cook provided this advice. Ms. Cook retorted that since we met, I had criticized Ms. Green, which made Ms. Green feel uncomfortable. I turned to Ms. Green and asked if this was true. Ms. Green confirmed that she felt I had targeted her all year and that she was extremely uncomfortable around me. I took a breath. I felt my face and ears become hot, red and blotchy, not because I felt guilty, but because I was taken aback. I was also perplexed. I did not understand how my interactions with Ms. Green had been so wildly misinterpreted. My sole intent in this conversation was to advocate for a student and suggest Ms. Green reflect on her tone and word choice. I could not recall another negative interaction I had had with Ms. Green that year. I looked at Ms. Green, and with all the compassion I could muster, told her that my intentions have never been to make her uncomfortable or to pick on her in any way. Rather, I was simply trying to provide some feedback to make her teaching practices stronger and her classroom environment more welcoming.

My conciliatory efforts only served as the kickstarter for Ms. Green's tears. Ms. Cook promptly concluded the meeting and made certain to tell me it was not in the least productive. The two women rose and walked out.

I had been an assistant principal for only a few months and that was one of my first attempts at an independent difficult conversation with a staff member. Instead of a successful, collaborative and open conversation, it was a one-sided combat zone and even waving the white-flag didn't save me. But wait, this story gets worse for my newly-not-even-minted-assistant-principal self. Ms. Green called in more troops. The next day, she sent the staff an email reporting that her conversation with me left her feeling so stressed and emotional that the heart rate of her unborn child plummeted dangerously low and that she had been required to be hospitalized last night. She alluded that my actions nearly caused a termination of her pregnancy, and even suggested that perhaps that was my true intention. And as if being known as a plotting and vengeful new assistant principal wasn't enough to deal with, I also received a call from the Equal Opportunity Compliance Office who cross-examined me about my actions during the feedback conversation and my treatment of a pregnant woman.

What kind of school was this? What was wrong with this staff? How could advocating for an autistic, transgender special education student be so misinterpreted? Is this how all staff members responded when asked to have a conversation with a member of the leadership team? What had I gotten myself into?

Did I really want to be a school leader after all?

My interaction with Ms. Green and Ms. Cook was indicative of the culture I walked into. The hatred and resentment toward the administrative team was palpable. Interactions between staff and administration was vitriol. A few staff members were actively working to remove the leadership team from their positions. A dark cloud of angst, unhappiness, and lethargy hung over the school causing even the most positive, joyful people to feel stifled and depressed. I was one of those positive, joyful people, so I know best of all how pollutive a culture like this could be to one's perspective of the glass being half full or empty. At the end of my first year at the school, my principal resigned. Newly-not-even-minted-assistant principal me was now the sole administrator in a building with 50 staff and 525 students. That summer, I was left to run the school by myself. Thirteen staff members resigned that summer. I had no partner to assist with interviewing and filling the vacancies. I had no partner in designing a vision for the year, planning opening week PD, balancing our $4 million budget, or helping me process the countless negative interactions I had experienced in my first year. Any positive thoughts I had were drowned by anxiety. Instead of hiring a full-time principal, my network assigned a retired, part-time administrator to work at the school a few days a week (who I didn't meet until the first week of school.). I was an assistant principal with one year of experience under my heels, but I was essentially left alone to run a school and a staff that, quite frankly, at the time, I hated.

Believe me, I spent several evenings with a glass of wine and Google while I searched for other jobs. But, no assistant principal positions in my district interested me and I was tired of transitioning. In the past four years I had worked at four different schools because I had transitioned from classroom teacher to graduate student to resident. Those reasons aside, I am still uncertain as to why I actually stayed. I rarely run from a challenge, but I also had never been unhappier in a school. Now, four years later, I am the proud principal of that same school, working with a staff I adore, and breaking school records in academics, athletics, and school culture.

My life coach worked diligently with me to determine the best next steps for me. She knew I was an energetic, optimistic, hard working woman who had a passion for providing equal educational opportunities for all children, regardless of race, ability, English proficiency, gender, or socioeconomic status. Once it became clear that I was going to stay, she asked me, "What do you need to transform this school into a place where you can live out your passion?" I immediately responded that the staff culture needed an overhaul. Over the next three years, I worked to transform the staff culture from toxic to tolerable to a true team. It started with developing and implementing four truths that any school can utilize as needed to change its culture: grace and gratitude to change mindsets, giving the voices of the strongest opponents a seat at the table, distributive leadership, and having difficult conversations.

First, I needed to transform my own mindset due to the hate and distrust I had experienced from staff members. This was challenging. I had to focus on the best in everyone. I had to set my negative experiences aside and lead as if it was New Years' Day: new year, new start, new me. Afterall, I still believe that the root of the staff's unhappiness was not feeling valued or appreciated. Staff needed a leader who believed that everyone had something to offer. So that became my new approach. I had to let go of the negative experiences of the prior year and operate with the mindset that everyone had strengths and their strengths could make our school a great place to work. I praised individual staff for their successes, showed gratitude often by thanking staff members publicly, put shout outs in the weekly bulletin, implemented a weekly award system in which staff members could honor their colleagues, squashed toxic energy with optimism, and displayed a great deal of grace in the most challenging, uncomfortable situations. I proved I would not be pulled to a toxic place and would continue to lead with joy and energy. Slowly, staff realized that I was not a wolf out to get them, but was truly invested in the good they had to offer the school. Staff members now refer to the times before this as "The Dark Ages" which tells me that they recognize the progress we made as much as I do.

The second truth I needed to embrace was that I needed to give my strongest opponents a seat with me at the table. Most of the staff had removed their stuck mindset that I was a vindictive she-devil, and I had removed my own mindset that most of the staff were stuck in their ways and would not adapt to change. Now it was time to work on my most veteran, toxic yet talented individuals if I was really going to turn the ship. For these folks, the hate, anger, and frustration with me and the administration in general was deeply rooted. When I became principal, I was their fifth principal in five years. The changes jaded them. They had lived through new visions, new routines, and new expectations every year for five years. They did not know who to believe or who to trust. I had to convince them that I would not abandon them and sink yet another year of dreams. Many of these veterans had strong classroom practices, robust, detailed plans, and years of experience working with many different types of learners. Their attitudes resisted me and my changes, but I needed to build trustworthy relationships with them so that we could pool our talents together to do transformative work for the school. They needed to know that not only did I recognize their talents, but that I wanted to leverage their strengths to help make improvements across the school. Therefore, I started to invite those talented yet toxic veterans to the table when I had to make difficult decisions so that I was not making school-wide decisions in isolation. My strong, trusting relationships with my new frenemies was epitomized during a heated discussion about whether to keep or abolish our 30-minute advisory block that ran four days a week. First, this advisory structure was not within district policy. 90 minutes of the week was unaccounted for instructional time and it put our bell schedule wildly out of compliance with required instructional minutes. It's a mystery how it was ever initially approved. It needed to go. I could have made that decision on my own, but I knew a unilateral decision like that might move the school into compliance, but it would also set back recent progress. I desperately needed the support of my most vocal and veteran staff members or I would dismantle all the relationship-building I had done over the past few years with that one decision. Therefore, I grew the conversation strategically. This proposed change was rooted in valid policies and evidence and I armed my argument with those facts. I started by talking individually with my new frenemies, key people who needed the information first, and needed to hear my message directly and not a message garbled through a game of telephone. Then, I approached small groups and leadership teams such as the ILT. Eventually, I hosted a whole-staff conversation. It was collegial, professional, and productive, and in the end the vast majority of staff members came to the needed conclusion-- the advisory program was against policy and had to go. A few years prior, this conversation likely would have cost me my job.

The third truth that transforms school culture is giving leaders a space to lead. Once staff understood that I was invested in their strengths, and once I had a few key stakeholders helping me make important decisions, I needed staff leaders to lead. In my second year at the school, I was an assistant principal without a principal. I needed help. I have never felt exhaustion like that which I felt as an assistant principal without a principal. I was tired. When my director would come for a walk-through, she would utter the phrase "Why are you taking on that task?" over and over again. Much of the trust-building I had done involved me taking over the work entirely. It was not sustainable. I had to shift my practice. I had to build trust by trusting that others could do and wanted to do high-quality work. Instead of being the sole leader, I needed to distribute the leadership. Eventually, I found that handing over good, challenging work to teacher leaders was one of the greatest trust building moves I made. I started by asking a few people with whom I had a trusting relationship to take on small teams-- serve on the instructional leadership team, lead 9th grade on-track work, or take on a few students for a check-in-check-out intervention, for example. When the school received record on-track rates as well as record attendance and graduation rates, everybody knew those teachers had been successful. Over time, a desire grew in others to take on a leadership role as they saw their colleagues boasting impressive results. Today, a staff member leads each grade level team and each department, a teacher serves as an instructional coach, another is the evening school coordinator, another is the look and feel coordinator, and the list continues.

Distributed leadership became contagious at our school. In my fourth year, all but two staff members supported an engagement outside of their job description. The culture shifted from I'm not doing anything for this school! What more can I do for our school? **Had I not shifted to a culture of distributed leadership, I may have been just** *another burnt out principal who moved on after a few years of leading.*

The fourth truth was one that I had to make peace with: some people did not want to be contributing members of the team. Either they did not want to see the school transform into a more positive, productive learning environment, or they did wish the best for the school but had been so hurt that it was time for them to move on. In two years, 25 staff members left. Most people chose to leave on their own, and I wished each of those people well in their new adventures. However, there were some staff members who I helped make the decision to move on. I did so by making them uncomfortable, not by embarrassing them, belittling them, or disrespecting them, but by engaging them in simple, open conversations. For instance, one staff member disappeared for a week and asked another staff member to serve as her messenger to relay why she was absent from school. She was too ill to call me on the phone, but not too ill to communicate with her colleague. It did not add up. That made for an uncomfortable conversation, but a necessary one. Another staff member lied about smuggling two unapproved volunteers onto a school field trip. That started another touchy conversation. And when another staff member was caught embezzling funds from our athletic department, I quickly turned that conversation over to the Illinois Inspector General. I learned that I did not need to become hostile or vengeful to ensure my staff upheld the highest levels of integrity. Rather, in the same manner adults often want their kids treated, I merely needed to converse with these adults when I observed questionable activities. For many of those staff, my knowledge of their inappropriate actions was enough for them to choose on their own to leave. After five years at the school, I have only evaluated out three educators. I had tough conversations when I had to, but I made sure that even in those tough conversations I showed a great deal of grace. My actions communicated that I act with integrity, and I expect the same integrity from my staff. This was the new culture and even if the choices people made were wrong, they deserved no less respect during these conversations. While I spent two summers interviewing, hiring and rebuilding a staff, and while that was not easy work, today, I can say with confidence that every leave had a purpose, and I wish each person success in their new adventures.

My leadership journey is rooted in the work of shifting staff culture. The work--and it was work-- required more patience and grace than I knew I had. In the thick of it, I recall being frustrated that so much of my time was spent on adults-- their behaviors, attitudes and relationships--instead of kids. Now, in year five, I realize that the children are happier, safer, and engaged in more meaningful learning because the adults who serve them are happier, safer, and engaged in meaningful work. Early in my teaching career I was taught that teacher actions drive student actions: that student actions are a result of the expectations of the adult standing in front of them. What my journey has taught me is that leader actions drive teacher actions which drive student results. Our school is the school it is today because of my transformational leadership.

About Lydia Ryan

Lydia Ryan *was born in Chicago, IL and raised in the south suburbs. She is the proud life partner of Mike Menzer, daughter to two loving parents, and best friend to an older brother and younger sister.*

As a first generation female college student, Lydia attended Purdue University in West Lafayette, IN, where she earned a bachelor's degree in Secondary English Education. Upon graduation, Lydia became a high school English teacher in Chicago Public Schools. She proudly and joyfully served students on the far northwest and west sides of the city. Lydia then moved to Boston to earn her master's in School Leadership from the Harvard Graduate School of Education. Upon graduation, she returned to Chicago Public Schools where she served as an assistant principal for two years. She is now in her third year as the proud principal of Chicago Academy High School on the far northwest side: a small, diverse, caring community that Lydia is grateful to call home. In 2018, Lydia was asked to serve on the Principal Advisory Committee for Chicago Public School's Chief Executive Officer, Dr. Janice Jackson. In 2019, Lydia was named a lead principal for the Academy for Urban School Leadership (AUSL) network in Chicago Public Schools.

Lydia is proud of the work she has done at Chicago Academy to improve student and staff feelings of safety and organization. Her focus on school culture, relationships, and trust resulted in moving the school's organization rating to the highest level in just one year. She has led her community to record high on-track, graduation, and attendance rates. Under Lydia's leadership, Chicago Academy High School has two active parent groups, the first in CAHS's history.

She is also proud of creating and supporting highly effective teacher teams and developing the capacity of staff members to lead those teams.

Lydia is a yogi and a runner and likes to cook, travel, and read. Lydia would not be the leader she is today without the mentorship of strong female leaders including Susan Lofton, Dr. Annise Lewis, Dr. Lynda Williams, and Pamela Cook.

Dr. Amy Miller

You cannot always control what goes on outside. But you can always control what goes on inside." -Dr. Wayne Dyer

CHAPTER 8

WORK-LIFE BALANCE

By Dr. Amy Miller

Hard work and creativity is in my DNA. It's no wonder my life took the path that it did. As a little girl, my first role models were my parents. My earliest memories with my father included time spent at his car dealership answering phones and washing cars and my earliest memories of my mother were doing creative things like stenciling and learning to sew.

Many days in my childhood were also spent on our family's farm. While on the farm, I often spent time with my aunt, who was a teacher. As I grew into my middle school years, I often rode to school with her and helped in her classroom before school, after school, and in the summer. It was because of those experiences that I chose to become an educator.

In 1997, I enrolled as a freshman at a local university. I set out to get a degree in elementary education, but was given the last-minute opportunity to add special education and finish in four years since the university was starting a new dual degree option. I had zero experience in special education and was a bit nervous about this option, but figured it would help my chances of getting a job. Little did I realize it would become a primary focus in my educational career.

My first semester in college was a whirlwind. I was on a cheerleading scholarship, adjusting to living on my own, "socializing" too much, and struggling academically for the first time in my life. Through my K-12 career, I had very little need to study as things came very easily to me. I was enough of a people-pleaser to be able to do the minimum, get good grades, and keep teachers and my parents off my back. I was a gifted student, so I would occasionally hear, "I expect more from you" from my teachers and parents, which was enough to light a fire under me every so often.

But when I received my first semester grades, things got real. My whopping 2.0 quickly landed me into a three-hour mandatory study hall, nightly, to keep my cheerleading scholarship. It also caused my father to give me an ultimatum of "4.0 from this point forward or you're coming home". I heard both messages loud and clear and I kept my end of the bargain clear through graduation. This lesson has served me well many times in my career.

My very first teaching interview led to my very first teaching job. I don't remember much about the interview itself but what I remember very clearly was the connection I made with the superintendent, who just happened to be the longest tenured superintendent in the history of Pennsylvania. He was friendly and fun and I felt as though he appreciated my spunk and enthusiasm. A positive work environment was very important to me, so I was 100% all in.

I was hired as a special education teacher for students in grades K-2. I really enjoyed the creativity and camaraderie which came with the position. I met some of the best educators during my years teaching.

It was truly a top-notch school district. But, I quickly realized that I was craving more leadership. I decided to go back for my master's degree in my second year of teaching. After that, I decided to continue my graduate education and complete my principal certification and special education supervisor certification.

Both the principal certification and the special education certification required internships and the superintendent took me under his wing to be sure that I had the best experience possible. He not only spent time mentoring me, but he gave me access to his team of administrators. The relationships and experiences I gained during my internships were priceless in my career.

Soon after my internships, I applied for a 10-month position as an assistant middle school principal in a nearby school district. I interviewed and accepted the position, at the young age of 25, which served as a stepping stone for me into my position as Special Education Director the following year. When I transitioned into the director position, I negotiated the contract to make the position 10-months because I was newly married and had not yet started a family.

I remained in the director position for four years. The position was a great place for me to become a solid administrator. I wasn't in the thick of building level responsibilities and daily discipline. Instead, I had a nice balance of staff and student interaction and was able to watch and learn how the school district operated, K-12. Sure, there was conflict and problem-solving but I never felt like I was on my own because I worked so closely with the other administrators.

During my time as director, I was able to see the inner workings of the school district on a closer level than other administrative positions. My office was in the central office, but my daily routine included getting out to each of the buildings for meetings and teacher observations. I also traveled outside of the school district and made connections with other public schools, private schools, and other service providers such as mental health and behavioral support agencies. I attended more professional development during those years than all other years combined. It was such a great proving ground for me.

During my time as director, I also continued my education to add my Superintendent Letter of Eligibility to my certification. Being a superintendent was not something I saw in my future, but I thought it was the next natural step in my education, especially since I had a goal of earning my doctorate degree in the future.

In my last year as the director, our school district was facing some turbulence with the resignation of our superintendent and sudden budgetary stress from the state. I unexpectedly ended up taking on the position of Acting Superintendent until we could advertise and hire for the position. I was 30 years old when I stepped into this position and I had a seven month old baby at home. I was assured that I would primarily be the "face" of the school district but others behind the scenes would help out significantly.

Prior to our superintendent resigning, the District made plans to furlough 12 full-time teachers and I was left dealing with the brunt of the fall out from that situation. My first school board meeting, which I was in charge, included a packed cafeteria with teaching staff and community members upset with the recent furlough announcement. It was heated, contentious, and stressful--but also a great experience. I also had the experience of teacher negotiations during my tenure and saw the behind-the-scenes process of the collective bargaining agreement.

At the time we hired a new superintendent, we also had the retirement of our elementary principal, who supervised two elementary buildings. With the teacher cuts also came administrative cuts, so I found myself with virtually two jobs. I took over one of the elementary buildings and our curriculum director took over the other building. My first year in this role was very difficult. I was my own worst enemy as the role of special education director required me to be "out and about" and the role of the principal required me to be inside the school building and "visible". After a year of that struggle, the District allowed me to have a special education coordinator position in order to distribute the workload to a more reasonable pace. This worked well and allowed me to still keep a pulse of the special education department while also allowing me to focus on my elementary building.

After a few years as building principal, I decided to pursue my doctorate degree. It was something I always had in the back of my mind as a goal, but one that I wasn't sure how to accomplish with my already busy life. At that point, we had two little girls at home and I didn't want to interfere with family time as it had always been a high priority for me. In the back of my mind, I felt like a doctorate degree would give me options beyond public school in the event that I didn't wish to advance my career further than a building principal.

The classes were held on Tuesday nights with multiple weekend classes throughout the first year of the program. I was accustomed to school board meetings on Tuesday nights so the program was a decent fit for our family's schedule. The workload which came with the program was heavy and I had to prioritize my time to accomplish the tasks and keep my sanity. I would typically do my work on Friday nights from about 7PM through 2AM. I continued this pattern clear through my dissertation and it worked out great because I was able to enjoy my weekends with the bulk of my work completed in one evening, after the girls were in bed.

Graduating with my doctorate was one of the highlights of my educational career. The caliber of people I was able to connect with was priceless and the feeling of completion was overwhelming. They call it an "end degree" because it symbolizes reaching the end of the road in continuing education.

It may have been the end of the road for me as a student, but it was just the beginning for me as a professor. I was able to begin teaching graduate education courses, as an adjunct professor, soon after I finished my degree and I have continued to teach multiple courses both in-person and online. The amazing part of it all is that I am working at the same university in which I was an undergraduate and graduate student. One of my favorite courses I teach is the special education supervisor practicum. It's such a unique experience to be teaching the courses which I previously took as a student. But what I love most about it is the opportunity to be an advocate and line of support for blossoming leaders.

Along with teaching at the collegiate level, I also take great pride and responsibility in mentoring aspiring principals and have hosted several of them, as interns, bringing them into the fold of my everyday life as a principal. I try to model a style and atmosphere of love, humor, and a hefty dose of hard work.

Outside of education, I have other outlets which fulfill my need for creativity and entrepreneurism. If you have a creative mind, you know what I'm talking about--the innate need to fulfill your ideas. My creativity often keeps me up at night as I'm planning out my latest project. I am often upcycling anything I can get my hands on. I love making trash into treasure, especially with furniture. I'm that person who stops for a roadside rescue and makes it into something amazing. I'm an avid thrifter and enjoy creating a wardrobe of sustainability and fashion. I often get compliments on my clothing and 99% of the time I respond with "Oh, I thrifted it from somewhere!". It's like a treasure hunt for me.

Four years ago, I chose to join a teacher friend in a network marketing skincare business. It sounded fun to promote products that I love in exchange for a discount and maybe some extra income. Growing up in our family business, I always valued entrepreneurism and loved the idea of limitless success. In my position as principal, there is no opportunity to earn extra income, trips, or other rewards so I liked the idea of joining a side business which allowed for these opportunities. It turned out to be far more than I expected it to be and I have enjoyed all of the perks of the business because I ran with it and saw the opportunity to grow at any rate I chose. Many educators are driven by achievement so these types of opportunities typically serve high achievers very well. Don't knock them until you give them a chance! I found a new lease on life by digging into personal development through my side gig. It's grown me, personally, far more than I ever anticipated.

Through personal development, I have recognized the need for self-care in my life. I now recognize that my hard-work, determination, and need for achievement comes with the cost of exhaustion and overwhelm. We are not designed to be in high-gear our whole lives. I always prided myself in continuing the family belief system that hard work is a status symbol and way of life. Now I am understanding that hard work is important, but equally so is the need for play and rest. Living full-speed ahead all of the time comes with consequences such as the breakdown of the body and mind--and I was beginning to see those effects.

I am a work in progress, but now prioritize my time and include daily practices of quieting my mind and distancing myself from situations which no longer serve me in a good way. I used to thrive on stress as a way of life but now that I know what a calm, quiet body and mind feel like, I crave that feeling instead. Sometimes it's hard to distance myself from conflict, especially in my line of work. It's a conscious effort on my part, but one that I hold as a high priority.

I'm still writing my story as I find the balance between career life and creative life. I find myself having dreams of a different life separate from the daily grind, yet I enjoy the challenges of the principalship.

My career has certainly been scattered with challenges along the way. I've been asked many times for advice to navigate education as a woman in a leadership position. My advice is to learn to play the game. Changes in education are constant and changes in leadership are inevitable. Embrace the changes and enjoy the challenges as those are what grow strong leaders who are not afraid. Be aware of the people who you hold close and be even more aware of your words. They both have profound power to influence your heart and your mind--both of which are paramount in a position of leadership.

About Dr. Amy Miller

Dr. Amy Miller *is an educator with a strong passion for positive psychology and leadership. Amy has spent the last 19 years in public education, 14 of which have been in administration. Miller has held roles including special education teacher, assistant principal, special education director, and acting superintendent. Amy is currently an elementary principal; a role she has held for the last 9 years.*

Beginning her administrative career at the early age of 25, Miller has a distinct desire to mentor new leaders and share her experiences with others. She does this through hosting principal interns, speaking engagements, and teaching at the university level. Amy enjoys studying the behavior of leaders which is evident in her 2016 research study, Are Resilient Principals More Committed to Their Work?: A Quantitative Study of Resilience and Work Commitment Among Principals in Pennsylvania.

Dr. Miller has an entrepreneurial spirit which she expresses through creative outlets including her skincare business and upcycling just about anything she can find. Miller refers to herself as a "thrifty-upcycler trapped in a professional's body". She loves adventure, trying new things, and meeting new people. Amy is known for her music videos she creates for fun announcements for students and parents throughout the school year.

Dr. Miller resides in Pennsylvania with her husband and two young daughters.

Amena Moiz

"We are an amalgamation of our experiences: the commendable, the erroneous, and the traumatic. We would not be the leaders we are today were it not for those experiences."

- A. Moiz

CHAPTER 9

LEAPS OF FAITH

By Amena Moiz

"Do not follow where the path may lead. Go instead where there is no path and leave a trail."
-Ralph Waldo Emerson

In the name of God, the Beneficent, the Merciful. This quote by Emerson exemplifies the purpose of anyone who takes on leadership. I have the utmost respect for those of us who are trailblazers in education because there is rarely a time when we are not faced with difficult situations. I have felt a sense of accomplishment and joy in this position along with bearing a burden of responsibility that is under constant scrutiny not only from outside but also from within.

As I study my greatest challenge and look back at the past several years, I discovered that they consist of a series of leaps of faith that are highlighted throughout my journey and developed into five leadership lessons: being resilient, having champions, acknowledging setbacks, reflecting honestly and valuing my experience. These five lessons have allowed me to embrace my current principalship by helping me to process painstaking heartbreak, overcoming self doubt and compelling me to rise to the level of leadership that my students and staff deserve.

The leader I am today is rooted in how I was raised, continues with my foray into school administration, loses momentum when faced with my greatest challenge as a school leader and culminates in reflective growth.

Foundation

My journey begins with my parents' resilience, reverence for their teachers and a desire to empower us through education. They took a leap of faith and immigrated to America from India in 1974 while in their early 20s. Later in life we would learn of their sacrifice and struggles in leaving their families, friends and everything they knew behind to go to a new country thousands of miles away motivated and driven by the desire for a better education. When my parents shared stories of their many childhood adventures, there was always a sparkle in their eyes as they reminisced about school. The respect and deference they had for their teachers was unflinching. There was never a question that myself and my siblings would graduate high school, go on to college and earn a degree. I distinctly remember finding it puzzling when my peers would tell me how they were unsure of their post high school plans and the affirmations I would receive from teachers when they would ask what I wanted to do as a career choice while still in middle school. As I reflect on this, I believe that being raised with this focus on education could have been the early seeding of my desire to be a teacher.

I have been in love with teaching for as long as I can remember, much to the chagrin of my siblings. I was always good with younger kids and enjoyed being around them. I distinctly recall playing school with my younger siblings after my mom had taken us school shopping. The anticipation and excitement of picking out every item I needed and didn't, coming home and taking everything out of its packages, sorting and rearranging them into a new pencil box, the intoxicating smell of new crayons and erasers and let's not forget the infamous trapper-keeper. The cherry on top: having both of my siblings sitting in front of me while I told them what to do, my version of being a teacher back then. They would always revolt and ask me why I was the only one that could be the teacher and not them. It makes me smile now. I was quite the bully to my sister and brother, like any good older sibling aspires.

My vision for my profession caused me to be resolute and true to my passion. When my parents were growing up in India and before they immigrated, engineering and medicine were the two main fields of employment that students in their town strived for and could be successful at in making a decent income. That same thinking was fostered with us from an early age. I knew I was passionate about teaching but in the back of my mind, I also knew that my parents wanted me to become a doctor. I went ahead and enrolled in college with the intent to major in the sciences and go onto medical school. After my first semester, I decided that I really didn't want to go into medicine. I wanted desperately to become a teacher and decided to take a leap of faith. I was determined to make education my reality. One night as I was helping set the dinner table with Indian food that my mom had cooked, not even the tantalizing and mouth-watering smell of rice, daal and a spinach and meat salan could help keep my stomach from being in knots. This was the night I chose to do my version of a big reveal. As we were eating dinner and conversing about our day, I announced to my parents that I wanted to change my major from pre-med to education. It took all the courage I could muster to have this conversation because I knew it was important to them and was anticipating their disappointment. After I made my statement, a pall cast over the dinner table and we finished eating in silence. After having further conversations, my parents were on board. They weren't thrilled at the time about my decision but were supportive and knew how passionate I was about education from what they observed in me as a child.

Champions

Because of my dedication towards education, I tended to gravitate towards others of the same belief and drive. I never had any administrative aspirations. I knew that I had leadership skills but didn't think of ever pursuing that path. I was confident that I would retire from teaching. I didn't realize that a simple text late one evening could have such a profound impact in ways that I could never imagine.

I was in my car after picking up my husband from the airport and I got a text from one of my former principals. The words, "would you be interested in applying for a middle school dean (assistant principal) position?" staring back at me. At first I thought that it was an error and was accidentally sent so I brought it to her attention but then she restated her original question. I remember feeling startled. Administration? Me? A myriad of thoughts and ideas were jumbled and rushing through my head. I immediately turned to my husband and asked for his opinion because he was my sounding board. He said what he always says "if you want to do it, I will support you". I expressed my concern about moving again, displacing our son and living apart. With a reassuring tone he said "we will figure it out".

And with those words, my inner monologue began: Oh my God, an administrator? Can I do it? Am I capable? Do I want to do it? Can I leave the classroom and my students? What did my former principal see in me that led to me receiving this text? Sassy Sally was my term of endearment for my former principal and boy was she was a force to be reckoned with. I have nothing but respect and admiration for her. I worked as a science teacher one and a half years earlier at her school. We had a wonderful teacher-principal relationship that evolved into more of a friendship and mentoring role. At the end of that school year I approached her expressing my desire to relocate so that my son and I could be closer to my husband

and not have to live apart due to employment locations. She was incredibly supportive especially when I shared that I was anxious about trying to find employment in that particular city again due to my prior experience of being rejected as a Muslim woman who wore hijab (head scarf) and anticipated it would be a struggle. She immediately picked up the phone and contacted the principal of the other school where I had applied for a science teaching position and weaved into her conversation that I was Muslim and wore hijab and boldly asked if that would be an issue. The principal said it wasn't going to be an issue and he was looking forward to meeting me. I remember being so relieved and now as I look back, recognizing her brazenness and fortitude as a female administrator. She had this way of making a person feel heard and holding them to high expectations simultaneously. She was also the same person who had sent the text and that meant the world to me. If I were to win this opportunity, it would separate our family again. After talking in more detail with my husband and praying on it, I called and had a conversation with my former principal. She walked me through why she thought I would make a good leader and the next steps in the interview process. I took a leap of faith and was hired into an administrative role which eventually led to a principalship a few years later and one of the biggest challenges I faced as a school leader. I would not be where I am today were it not for the support and guidance of my husband and Sassy Sally's confidence and faith in my ability to lead a building of students and staff. They were my champions for which I am eternally grateful.

Full Circle

Getting up after falling down is easier said than done. To be honest, it took me nearly 4 years to accomplish this after a devastating moment in my career. It started and ended at Panera.

This particular Panera held pleasant, happy memories, but not this time. Not this day. I tried to find a spot that was discreet enough to give some privacy but also lit by windows so I wouldn't feel like I was going to suffocate. The director walked in, quickly scanned the area, found the booth, unbuttoned his jacket and sat down. He and I both studied each other, belaboring the inevitable. Fighting back tears and trying my best to keep my composure, I listened. Things aren't going well, he said and at that moment I looked down transfixed on the broccoli and cheese soup bread bowl in front of me. Comfort food I thought, it'll help I'm sure. It didn't. I could hear him say that the student growth data isn't where it should be and that I was making mistakes due to impulsive decision making and in an instant I had a flashback to March 2012, two years earlier. It was hiring day. I found a nice round table and laid out my things. I had my binder and interview questions ready to go. I had read multiple books on the best techniques and strategies and what qualities and characteristics to look for in a candidate. I collaborated with other principals. I knew what I was seeking and determined to find the right fit. I came an hour early so I could be well prepared and rehearsed. I was at this exact same Panera, interviewing for two office positions for my yet to be renovated school building where I was going to have my first principalship and be the founding principal of that school. Interview after interview, candidate after candidate, it wasn't clicking. Then, I found two perfect people that I knew would bring joy to my students and families as well as structure to the office. I immediately offered them positions. I was ecstatic, full of hope and optimism about this tremendous responsibility that was placed on my shoulders. I was fortunate enough to be able to build my vision for my school and then see that through. I couldn't wait to open our doors and welcome my students and staff. It was going to be epic. A day that was in stark contrast to today.

The loud clink of a spoon hitting a bowl jarred me back to the present. He continued talking about the student achievement data and then proceeded to give me two options: I could resign and look for other job opportunities or I would find myself unemployed in

June. Needless to say, I definitely wasn't anticipating hearing the latter two years into my principalship. I will give you some time to think about it he said and then he left, just like that. I sat there blinking back tears but it was hopeless. It was as if a floodgate had opened. Two years. My school was only two years old. What about my students? My staff? Families? Community? What about those relationships that were built that would provide enriching experiences to my students? Who was going to replace me? Were they going to be good to my students and staff? What will they change about the culture we were building? Two years and I felt like my heart was being ripped out of my chest because I took pride in serving and making a difference in my students' lives and now it was all being taken away from me. This overwhelming feeling was difficult to process. One tear then two then I couldn't stop. I was quietly sobbing. I closed my eyes and put my head against the back of the seat. What am I going to do now? What did I do to deserve this? How did I get here? How could they take away the one thing that was my blood sweat and tears? Where do I go from here? Little did I realize that this experience would be the biggest motivator for my next principalship.

Resilience

It's an understatement to say that this was a devastating moment in my career. I knew God had a plan but it was very difficult for me to look beyond myself. I had this gnawing feeling of utter worthlessness because I felt that I had failed my students and my staff. I felt like I had nothing to offer and went into a deep depression. I went on to take an assistant principal position within the same district for the next three years. I was struggling because I felt like a candle that was snuffed soon after it was lit, not even having enough time to warm the wax. During this time as an assistant principal, I distinctly remember when the director of my school asked me why I didn't venture out and try something new in a different district. This thought had unnerved me. I told him I wasn't interested and that I would rather stay because I was comfortable and knew what to expect. I will never forget what he said next: a person can only continue growing if they are uncomfortable. The following year I took a leap of faith and was ready to leave and take on something new and challenging. Truth be told, I also recognized that due to my anger of what happened three years earlier, I was doing a disservice to my current students and staff because I was unwilling to let go thereby unable to be the best version of myself as a leader. I felt that I had been wronged years before but if I am being honest with myself I was wallowing in self-pity. I knew my data and student growth along with my enrollment wasn't where it needed to be and that second year because I was feeling this relentless pressure to perform I started making decisions under duress. I know I made mistakes in my brief stay as a principal, giving new meaning to the phrase 'I don't know what I don't know' but was it all really that bad? Was I truly doing a disservice to my students? I don't take that statement lightly. A couple of years ago I started to realize that those two years were imperative to my leadership journey. It also slowly started to dawn on me the tremendous achievements we made in those two short years: the culture we built, the community relationships we fostered, the awards our school received after its first year, the families whose needs we were able to meet and above all the students we proudly served. I learned so much from the experience but it took me a while to understand and see it for what it was. As one of my friends stated, "Moiz, it's been a minute, let it go!"

Reflections

LIke I mentioned earlier, letting go took some time. I was at a place where I felt so defeated, I had nothing to give. It was weighing heavy on me and I knew I had to do something to relight the candle. For as much as I wanted a miracle to happen that would place me back in that building, I knew that wasn't a possibility. I had to reignite that flame because deep down I knew that I did have something to offer, I just had to prove it to myself. As a result of that desire, I applied for and was hired to take on a new principalship a little over two years ago. It has allowed me to use my skill set and past experiences to start building something special. I began to see my vision of success for my students and my team come to life again. Slowly but surely that fire was rekindled and I started regaining my confidence and embracing that excitement I had years before. I now feel empowered to drive initiatives for my students and staff with no hesitation and recognize the significance of continuing to seek out leadership growth opportunities for myself.

As I reflect on my journey, there are five leadership lessons that prominently stand out:

1. *Being resilient and staying true to my passion for serving my students.*

2. *Surrounding myself with champions who are there to guide and support me.*

3. *Experiencing a setback as a slight detour and continuing on my journey.*

4. *Reflecting and being honest with myself.*

5. *Valuing past experiences to guide my present while embracing future opportunities for success.*

As much as I hate to admit it, even with all that heartbreak, I would not change anything that has happened these past 19 years because I would not be the leader I am today were it not for those experiences: the commendable, the erroneous, and the traumatic. My passion and priority has always been serving my students and staff. I am dedicated to being their champion as others have been for me because they deserve nothing less. This tremendous responsibility has been my biggest motivator as I continue on this yet elusive leadership journey. I am eagerly awaiting my next leap of faith and where it will lead me.

About Amena Moiz

Mrs. Amena Moiz *was born in Wyandotte, Michigan to Indian immigrants and is the oldest of three siblings. After graduating from the University of Michigan-Flint, she began the first few years of her educational career at a local Islamic school. Over the next nineteen years she proceeded to work as a middle school science teacher, assistant principal and principal in inner-city urban charter schools in Detroit, Flint, Holland, Grand Rapids and Muskegon.*

Mrs. Moiz was the founding principal of a school that was recognized for Employee Engagement and Parent Satisfaction. She served as a graduate instructor at the University of Michigan-Flint for the Master of Arts teacher Certification program. She currently works as a Middle School Principal in Grand Rapids, Michigan and is in her fourth year as an adjunct faculty member of the Johns Hopkins School of Education Master's of Science in Education program. She also serves on the board of the Islamic School of Grand Rapids and recently completed the Women in Education Leadership Institute at the Harvard Graduate School of Education.

Mrs. Moiz completed her Bachelors of Science. in Education at the University of Michigan-Flint along with her Masters of Arts. in Early Childhood Education. She most recently completed her Masters of Arts in Educational Leadership from Central Michigan University.

Mrs. Moiz has been married for 22 years and has one son, Noor, who recently turned 19 and is an entrepreneur growing a business he established as a junior in high school.

Mrs. Moiz would love to hear from you! Connect with the author:

Amenamoiz76@gmail.com

Mrs. Moiz is thankful to God for giving her this opportunity and to her champions for supporting her educational journey:

Anjum Moiz
Mohammad Moiz
Scott Carvo
Noor Carvo
Linda Caine-Smith
Shawn Leonard
Randy Rodriguez
Mr. Ley
Mr. Jackson

Charlene Saenz-Quarles

"We rise by lifting others." -Robert Ingersoll

CHAPTER 10

I AM ENOUGH

By Charlene Saenz-Quarles

Where do I begin...? I am a 34-year-old proud Latina and my journey as a mother, wife, and educator has been one of much patience, undying hope, strong faith, and self-growth. I have been fortunate to have inspirational mentors and an encouraging family which have been essential to me reaching my ultimate goal and dream of serving as a high school principal. Why a high school principal you may ask? As a high school student, I felt invisible, no matter how much I tried to fit in. I felt as though I was not "cool" enough to be a part of the popular social groups and not talented enough to be a part of a respected extracurricular group. The most difficult aspect of my high school journey as I look back and reflect is that I still carry some of that self-doubt with me till this day, that feeling that I'm not good enough. Now, as a high school principal, I am committed to recall upon my experience and try to be who I needed growing up, an educator who saw me for me and helped me grow. As I think back, I remember a young girl who graduated high school early to try and get a head start on life trying to navigate through her post-secondary education as a future first-generation college student and feeling lost and frustrated. Not knowing where to begin nor how, for so many reasons. This state of confusion does not necessarily go away throughout life, but just becomes a little less foggy and you learn how to light your path with those around you.

I began my college education at local community colleges, transferred after two years after working in retail and product promotion. I continued my studies at a local California State University and had a blast! I finally felt like I belonged. I met incredible people and became involved in the Foreign Language Department's editorial magazine as Co-Editor. I worked three jobs to help ease the financial burden on my parents. I worked at the local university bookstore, and two retail stores. By this time, I had my beautiful daughter, Bella and she was only one years old. My grandma, Rosa and parents helped care for my daughter while I attended school. It was during my undergraduate studies at the university that I landed my first foundational job in education serving as a Bilingual Clerk in an urban K-4 preparatory school in the city of San Bernardino. This school served a diverse low-socioeconomic student population and I was a part of the team who was on staff the first year it opened. I met some extremely influential people in that role, however, there was one, in particular, my principal. A young, male first-year principal who gave me any opportunity I could ask for. I shared with him that I too aspired to be a young principal like him someday. He saw the "ganas[1]" and the commitment I had towards achieving my dream and he taught me to work beyond expectations. To strive to stand out and recognize that it would take a lot of work and sacrifice, but if it's something I truly wanted I would work hard for. He provided me the opportunity to serve as a mentor to young female students on campus and connect with parents at school events. He made me feel like my role on campus was important, and that the impact I could

---

[1] *the want, the willingness to work hard*

make was immeasurable regardless of my professional title. He was my first mentor, the one who helped me build my confidence and pushed me to strive for excellence each and every day. He taught me what it truly meant to work as a team and to recognize and appreciate everyone's role because they are crucial to a school's success. I confided in him as I continued through my journey, through every position from teaching to administration and he always offered the same advice to go beyond expectations because only there will I be noticed and reach a true level of excellence.

I then had the pleasure of serving as a Spanish teacher in a suburban high school in Moreno Valley and I met the most amazing students who taught me that it was okay to be myself and connect with them, to let them see me, for me. As a first-year Spanish teacher at the age of 21, I learned the immense impact I could make on my students simply by noticing them, by taking the time to greet them every morning and being there every day after school or during lunch so they always had a safe and comfortable space to go to. Relationships are everything and they are essential when you serve, as an educator. *In getting to know my students I identified the needs that existed for the specific population for which I served. Many of my students were upperclassmen and faced financial hardship, as prom season approached many were excited to attend but could not afford to do so. Therefore, I collaborated with community members, parents and students to host, "The Pretty in Pink Boutique", a boutique that would open after school in the cafeteria for a few hours a week prior to prom. This boutique provided formal wear, alterations, hair, makeup, nails, and jewelry for students who couldn't afford prom. It was beautiful. Families would come in to shop with their high school students and they were ever so grateful. I had students excited to volunteer and bring other students in to help them shop. This was an unforgettable experience. I had plans to continue to grow the boutique the following year, to include items for males as well, and partner with additional community members, but I unfortunately, experienced uncertainty with my position at the end of that school year due to financial cuts within the district. This was devastating for me because I felt so connected to my students, colleagues, and school community.*

However, this unfortunate circumstance led me into another opportunity, to teach in a suburban high school in Yucaipa, and would later introduce me to my next mentor and the magnificent world of school administration. While teaching Spanish in Yucaipa I also served as the Dance Team Advisor and Administrative Designee. I worked with a very different student population then I was accustomed to, which presented many challenges for me. I went from teaching at a school that was racially diverse with a large Hispanic population to one that was not as such. I don't want you to think I am saying this to be negative, that is not my intent at all, and I need to make that clear. I point this out because it was a real challenge for me. I had to learn how to connect with a student population and school community that I could not necessarily identify with. Therefore, I became more involved on campus to submerge myself into the culture. I became the Dance Team Advisor. I lead a diverse Dance Team which brought together many groups that were not likely to work together from across the campus and students who felt like they did not belong, and we became a family. We transformed the school culture, we had a variety of ethnicities, genders and backgrounds on our team. I had to be their rock, their mentor, and their friend and they in turn trusted me and we excelled together. This was a very personal trial for me because my team went through very difficult situations and I had to uplift them during these moments and encourage them to not give up. Most importantly I had to demonstrate perseverance through my actions and leadership. I had to "walk the walk" and when I fell short, I had to "own it" and that was very difficult to do when 40 plus eyes are staring back at you but we did so together. You must always strive to lead by example, to own your faults and move forward. *Until this day I feel such honor and gratitude for having the opportunity to work with that team, through their perseverance I was reminded that with love and passion, I could do anything.*

After my second year of teaching at Yucaipa I was offered a position to serve as an Administrative Designee, and it was through this role that I was able to meet my second mentor. He was an Assistant Principal who took me under his wing and allowed me to take on roles that pushed me to rise to the challenges presented before me from managing student discipline situations, irate parents, habitual truant students, master schedule, and community relations. I would conduct home visits twice a week and learned how powerful and influential it was for me as an educator to see where my students came from and I learned how important it is to partner with parents as I strived to strengthen the school's English Learner Advisory Committee (ELAC). The daily conversations, reflections, and shadowing of my second mentor were inspiring and essential in preparing me for my next role.

In 2014 I obtained my role as an Assistant Principal at a high school in Ontario, it was incredible, and I was so excited! However, the reality was that I was a 26-year-old Latina and first year administrator with only five years of teaching experience, who was I to think I could do this at such a young age and so inexperienced, or so they said. I know I've mentioned this before but that's because the challenges that come along with being a young Hispanic woman in a role of authority and leadership are very real and darn right tough! I faced immense self-doubt and doubt from the staff, as well, but I "rolled with the punches" and made a decision to do whatever it took to succeed. But what does success really mean? I have decided that success is measured by the mark I leave behind when I leave an organization. I can either be remembered for the love and dedication I exhibited for the organization and its people because of the everlasting relationships I built within it and my actions, or not, and I have chosen to always build and lead with my heart. *Every day I worked harder, hoping they could see my heart through my work. I came into an Assistant Principal position that was new to my district, one that focused on student intervention. I had to analyze systems and interventions in place that increased student achievement and improve them. As a new administrator, I approached this task completely wrong by thinking I knew what our school needed and how it was to be implemented, therefore, completely disregarding the current counseling staff and intervention teachers. Due to attempting to complete this task with no input from these key people my plan did not gain any buy-in and instead I met the most resistance I have ever encountered. I learned through this experience that it is crucial to identify the influencers on your campus and collaborate to accomplish a task or project or even gain support for a cultural or paradigm shift. Be patient and go slow to go fast, developing trust is critical.* I strongly believe that when you focus on inspiring others to find their greatness and lift them up, then and only then, can you truly lead.

After serving as an Assistant Principal for three and a half years within the Achievement Office, Discipline Office, and Instruction Office, I achieved my dream. I became a high school Principal at a neighboring school. I again was faced with entering this role at the young age of 32 with only a few years of experience from working in administration. Nonetheless, I was familiar with this challenge and was ready to face it head on. Understanding it would require me to work harder, make additional sacrifices and work to be a leader people can trust and confide in. One, who people believed truly loved serving as their principal. I have learned so much in the short time I have served as principal. I have learned that it's okay to not be perfect to admit my wrongs and faults and be vulnerable. *I've realized that my staff wants to know that I too am human, that I too like to have fun, that I cry, that I become frustrated and feel that my cup is empty from time to time. I need my students, and staff to see my heart, my undying commitment to their success. My undying commitment to our future.*

I am thankful for every position I have held in education and have learned much for every experience. One of the most important lessons I have learned is that you are more than your title. Anyone can have the title of a Principal but how you carry out that role is what is truly important. *The biggest challenge I have faced as an educator has been feeling like I've had to prove myself because of my age, ethnicity and gender. However, I rely strongly on my faith, prayer and exercise to help get me through some of my most stressful days and recall a verse that reminds me to remain focused and move forward. "For I know the plans I have for you, declares the Lord, plans to prosper you and not to harm you, plans to give you hope and a future" (Jeremiah 29:11, NIV). I often have to remind myself that I need to just be me and that I am meant to be in this role because I believe this is where God wants me to be. Therefore, it is my responsibility to be excellent every day because my staff and students deserve nothing less.* You don't need to be perfect; you just need to be *you*.

I would like to dedicate this chapter to anyone who has ever supported me. To my beautiful children, who don't quite understand why mommy comes home so late on most days or sometimes don't see her at all. I pray that the sacrifices I have had to make, most of all as a mother, will all be worth it, because I have inspired those whom I work alongside for the better (students, staff and parents alike). That people will remember me as an influential person in their lives, that I one day will be mentioned in their story. To my parents, sister and loving husband for always being there for me and being my constant reminder that I am enough and always have been.

About Charlene Saenz-Quarles

Mrs. Charlene Saenz-Quarles *was born in Huntington Park, California as a second-generation Mexican American. She was the first in her family to attend college. After graduating from California State University of San Bernardino, she began the first few years of her educational career serving as a Bilingual Clerk at a local middle school. Over the next ten years, she proceeded to work as a substitute teacher, high school Spanish teacher, dance team advisor, administrative designee, assistant principal and principal in suburban schools in San Bernardino, Moreno Valley, Yucaipa, Ontario, and Montclair.*

Mrs. Saenz-Quarles strongly believes in community partnerships to promote student success and provide access to opportunities. While serving as a Spanish teacher she developed a community initiative to provide young women facing financial hardship with the opportunity to attend prom by partnering with local business owners and community leaders within the Moreno Valley area. She served as a founding member of a district-level committee for a program developed to support unaccompanied and foster youth throughout her district titled Winter Wonderland. *She currently serves as the proud Principal of Montclair High School. This high school serves over 2,800 students and has been recognized as an AVID National Demonstration School, Title I School with Distinction, Gold Ribbon School, Golden Bell Award recipient, and a US News and World Report Silver Medalist. She also recently completed the Women in Education Leadership Institute at the Harvard Graduate School of Education.*

Mrs. Saenz-Quarles completed her B.A. in Spanish - Hispanic Literature, Language and Civilization at the California State University of San Bernardino along with her M.A. in Education from Azusa Pacific University.

Mrs. Saenz-Quarles recently married her longtime companion of 14 years and has two children, an 11-year-old daughter, Bella, and a 6-year-old son, Amon. Mrs. Saenz-Quarles is reminded by her daughter, Bella, that she is capable of achieving her dreams, as Bella aspires to be the first Mexican and African American woman president of the United States. Her son, Amon, also inspires her to remain confident and believe in herself, as he aspires to be the most handsome boy in the first grade.

Mrs. Saenz-Quarles would love to hear from you! Connect with the author: Cjsaenz09@apu.edu

Mrs. Saenz-Quarles is first and foremost thankful to God for giving her this opportunity and to her champions for supporting her educational journey:

My loving husband, Michael Quarles
My beautiful children, Bella and Amon
My parents, Isela and Carlos Saenz
My sister, Alesi Saenz
My mentor, Dr. Mathew Holton

Danielle Wallace

"Am I doing the right thing at the right time, in the right way for the right reason."

-Stephanie McConnell

CHAPTER 11

PURPOSE: YOU CAN RUN BUT YOU CAN'T HIDE

By Danielle Wallace

"If you want to go fast, go alone. If you want to go far, go together."
African Proverb

My leadership journey began the moment I recognized that there was an equity issue in my beloved elementary school. As a child I always knew I wanted to be a teacher. I was the little girl that played school from the time I got home until the time I went to bed. My younger brother endured many lessons against his will. We laugh about it now, but he really was my very first student. As the eldest child and the shyest person in the family I found my place in the world in the classroom. I craved my teachers' attention, not because I didn't get attention at home but simply because I loved the classroom experience. There was something magical that happened when my teachers led instruction. I knew in my whole being that I would one day create that same feeling in a classroom of my own.

God created the space for me to go back to that special place many years later to serve as a First Grade teacher. Walking in that first *year brought back so many memories. It was the way I remembered it yet for some reason also very different. As a child the classrooms were filled with a rainbow of children, some from very different backgrounds but nonetheless a rainbow. Now as a teacher, that same school had lost some of its color. Initially it didn't bother me. I was living the dream. Teaching some of the best and brightest in our district. Our Parent Teacher Organization was strong and our test scores were through the roof. Our after school events were always filled with parents and community members. So what was missing? Why was I still feeling dissatisfied? Prior to this teaching experience I taught in some pretty tough places. I taught in places where we never had enough: enough books, enough resources, enough parent engagement, enough time to move the academic needle. The feeling of lack was emotionally draining and honestly there were many days where I wasn't sure I was cut out for teaching. But yet, here I am working in this little slice of heaven and yet still dissatisfied. Why?*

That feeling of dissatisfaction was fueled by my biggest equity question at that time: how could two schools in the same school district be physically so close yet systemically so different? How could it be possible for one school to have so much and the other school to have so little? Both were publicly funded. Both were filled with young children who deserve a high quality education. Same superintendent, same yellow bus system, same school calendar but living worlds apart. The answer to this equity question would become a defining moment in my career. I was presented with an unusual leap of faith and I couldn't convince myself not to take it!

"I'd rather regret the risks that I take that didn't work out than the chances I didn't take at all." Simone Biles

Working in a large urban district often times afford teachers and teacher leaders with incredible opportunities to lead under special assignment. I was fortunate enough to be selected as part of a team of teachers that would go in and help to transform the educational experience in one of our lowest performing elementary schools. The superintendent had decided to make a change in leadership and structure at this particular school. This meant new administrator, new teachers and new instructional focus. Working in this school would prove to be the most impactful teaching experience I would have up to that point in my career. The redesign process was designed to give the students and the community a fresh start. The new administrator was experienced in the change process and was certainly up for the challenge of "righting" what for so long had been a sinking ship. I felt honored to have been selected for this team. I knew immediately that I was in great hands under the tutelage of this new principal. She was equally unassuming, stoic, highly skilled and covered in #blackgirlmagic!

For the next four years, I would study the leadership of this amazing principal, Mrs. D. I admired how she interacted with every student, every parent, every district leader and every community member. No matter the situation she rose to a level of excellence. She had a presence about her that could calm any storm. She held the highest of expectations for everyone on our team, from the teachers to the custodial crew. She was the modern day Joe Clark with no need for a bat. I was in awe and thoroughly enjoyed working on her team even when it was hard. And trust me, it was hard! We were charged with overcoming academic and social hurdles day in and day out. Yet her presence and her attitude said together we can do this. Deep down inside I knew that she believed in us more than we could ever believe in ourselves. That type of support and encouragement helped us to make major headway as a building. We had figured out a way to "right" the sinking ship.

"Surround yourself only with people who are going to take you higher." Oprah Winfrey

For the last 20 years I have had the pleasure to collaborate with some amazing women leaders. Some of them chose me and some of them I chose along my leadership journey. It took several years into my teaching career to recognize that I, too, was a leader. Initially I only saw myself as "just" a teacher. As we all know there is no such thing as being "just" a teacher. This revelation came to me while working under the dynamic leadership of Mrs. D. I vividly remember her calling me into her office after school and asking me "What is your five year plan?" Not only did this question catch me off guard, I literally had no idea as to why she was even asking me. Why would I have a five year plan? Doesn't she know I'm going to retire from the classroom? Why would she expect anything different from me? Not only did she expect BIG things from me, she expected me to expect BIG things from me. This was my professional turning point.

That simple conversation changed the trajectory for how I saw myself not only as a teacher but more importantly as a leader. I quickly began to get engaged with the larger work within my school and my district. I worked diligently to secure the position of schoolwide lead teacher which then led to me having the opportunity to leave the classroom for three years and participate in a teacher on assignment program. In this role I was able to lead as a Teacher Evaluator and as an Instructional Coach. As I began to make connections with other leaders outside of my school I began to have more of those simple conversations. What's next for you Danielle? Where do you see yourself in five years? What will be your lasting impact on this work? Through dialogue and self-reflection I became more intentional about who would have access to my sphere of influence. I developed my interpersonal skills by actively taking professional risks, stepping up as a committee leader, mentoring other future female leaders and attending as many professional conferences as possible.

Unchartered Territory

In 2013 I found myself back on the campus of the University of Cincinnati. I had fallen in love with Instructional Coaching and needed to solidify my position in Central Office. Rumor had it that in order to advance at the district level you needed to have your Administrative license. I certainly didn't want to be a Principal or so I thought. Nothing about the position seemed appealing. Who would want to work 50-60 hours a week? Who would want the sole responsibility of running a schoolhouse knowing every decision you made might be questioned or scrutinized? Certainly not me! But here I was actively participating in an Educational Leadership program. With every lecture, every assignment and every interaction with current educational leaders I was becoming more intrigued about the "big seat". My curiosity peaked after completing a shadowing opportunity with a close friend in a local urban middle school. At the conclusion of my visit she mentioned that there would be administrative openings within the district. I knew very little about the district but I also knew getting a position within my current big urban district would be quite challenging.

After applying for the position I made sure I went above and beyond to get noticed. Completing the online application wasn't going to work for me. I didn't want to be just another number. I had to get noticed. I took it upon myself to hand deliver my application. I attended their upcoming board meeting. I asked my friend who worked in the district any and everything. Always, always, always leverage your connections. It took a little time but I finally got the call to come in for an informal interview. I was excited but overwhelmingly nervous. I was intentional about dressing the part even incorporating their school colors within my attire. I learned a long time ago, you don't dress for the job you have. You dress for the job you want.

As I exited my vehicle I walked with confidence into the building. I knew going in that I was familiar with the current superintendent. He and I came from the same district and had at one point attended a few of the same professional development conferences. What I didn't know was that he and I would literally run into each other as I was entering the building for this interview. The first thing he said was 'Why are you here?" Naturally my response was "to hopefully get a job." To my surprise he then calls out to the HR Director "Hire her". Now of course getting the position wasn't that easy but I have no doubt that him knowing me helped me secure my spot in this competitive job market. He wasn't solely responsible for me getting the position but his vote of confidence helped to remind me that.

"God doesn't call the qualified. He qualifies the called."

When I started as principal in 2015 I had never been an assistant principal. I was thrilled for the opportunity but I was terrified at what my staff would think. Would they respect my authority as a novice principal having never been second in command? Would they wonder how and why I got the job over other candidates, some internal? Would they challenge me at every turn because of what appeared to be a lack of experience? I remember sharing some of these concerns with my superintendent and his response calmed all of my fears. Not only did he remind me that I wasn't given this position, I earned it. But more importantly he reminded me that I had done the work to be in position to lead at this level. For the last ten years of my career I had been more than a teacher. I had served as a School-wide Lead Teacher, a Teacher Evaluator, and an Instructional Coach. I had actively participated on school and district level committees. I had engaged in professional discourse with parents, community members, colleagues and district leaders. I had demonstrated success at every level except the principalship. Clearly it was my turn and my time. God knew long ago that I would be here. He created space and opportunity for me to learn and lead with those who would nurture me, develop me and those who would challenge me. Knowing that my journey had come full circle I was mentally prepared to have a seat at the table and continue to fulfill my purpose.

Principal Wallace

I have to admit I was terrified. You never fully understand the role of the principal until you are sitting in the seat. In my first year I learned what felt like a million and one life lessons on my feet. That very first life lesson happened on my very first day. It was a hot day in July and I had just received my keys to the building. Prior to this day I had only had minimal contact and interaction with the current staff. As I walked into the building and began unpacking my things I received a call from the head custodian. He informed me that the staff refrigerator was inoperable and wanted to know what I planned to do about it. Totally perplexed by the question, I asked him who's in charge of replacing it. He quickly reminded me that I am in charge, Wait, what? I am in charge of appliances? I thought I was in charge of children and adults. Little did I know that as of that day I would be in charge of any and everything.

"She remembered who she was and the game changed." Lalah Deliah

The world has never been quite ready for women in leadership. Men have held positions of power for so long they simply don't know what to do when there is a power shift. It absolutely amazes me that the number of female teachers far exceeds that of men yet those coveted positions of power are still heavily dominated by men. We all know as women that once we have an opportunity to sit at the table we have to be bold and sometimes brash. We have to lean in even when it's completely uncomfortable. I remember the first time a parent gave me the look of bewilderment when he realized that I was the principal. His body language suggested that he wanted control of the situation if for no other reason than the fact that he was a man. I vividly remember him informing me that he and his wife both held Master's degrees. As if that somehow afforded him the privilege to disrespect my teacher or worse me. I quickly, and with the utmost respect, reminded him that I held not one but two such degrees and that had no bearing on the issue at hand. He quickly changed his tone and his position. Women leaders must own who they are at all times. It is imperative to their career and their psyche. The moment we forget who we are, how hard we have worked and how many sacrifices we've made we lose. If nothing else, get you a tribe. Connect with those who have your back and allow them to remind you of your strength when you're feeling less than who you know you are.

"If you can't pay it back, pay it forward." Catherine Ryan Hyde

Five years later I am still leading with passion and purpose. I have experienced some amazing highs and some devastating lows. I could write a book on the things I've seen and heard from students (and adults). I absolutely love what I do and I count it a privilege to be doing it with grace and confidence. I won't lie, some days are downright hard. Some days I don't want to get out of my car because I'm unsure of what holy hell is awaiting me. But those days are few and far in between. When my confidence is shaken or my emotional elevator is on the basement floor I remember to think of that one student who will be waiting for me. Waiting for me to give a hug, a high five, a word of encouragement or a stern talking to. They need me to show up at full capacity even when I don't feel like it. They are my daily motivation to show up and show out in the name of excellence. So many amazing women leaders did that for me time and time again. I am able to do what I do and be who I am because they saw something in me and by choice they continually poured a bit of themselves into my leadership vessel. My leadership is a manifestation of years of sowing seeds. I am blessed and forever grateful for those who have laid a foundation, a blueprint of sorts for me and the tribe of women leaders who surround me, cover me, nurture me and challenge me to be greater than who I ever imagined I could be. Day in and day out I am reminded that the principalship *will never be easy but it will always be worth it!*

About Danielle Wallace

Ms. Danielle N. Wallace *has been an educational leader for over two decades. Key leadership roles include School-wide Lead Teacher, Teacher Evaluator, Instructional Coach, Curriculum Specialist, OAESA Zone Director and Principal. Ms. Wallace earned a B.S. in Montessori Education from Xavier University (1996) and two Masters in Education from the University of Cincinnati; Curriculum and Instruction (2002) and Educational Leadership (2014). She is marching toward her 25th year as an active member of Delta Sigma Theta Sorority, Incorporated. In her "free" time, she enjoys sharing her love of jewelry with her clients, maximizing quality time with her amazing teenage daughter and bonding with her sister circle.*

"If you're the smartest person in the room, you're in the wrong room." Unknown

VISIONARY AUTHOR
DR. SHARON H. PORTER

About Dr. Sharon H. Porter

Dr. Sharon H. Porter (Dr. Sharon), *educator, author, publisher, and host, is the President of SHP Enterprise, the umbrella entity of Perfect Time SHP LLC, the G.R.I.N.D. Entrepreneur Network, Write the Book Now!, and SHP Media and Broadcasting. She is the host of the I Am Dr. Sharon Show, Executive Director of the Next in Line to Lead Aspiring Principal Academy (APLA), founder of the non-profit Young Ladies Who L.E.A.D. and Co-Founder, owner, and Editor-In-Chief of Vision & Purpose (V&P) LLC LifeStyle Magazine and Media.*

Dr. Sharon is a graduate of Howard University, Walden University, Johns Hopkins University, National-Louis University, and Winston-Salem State University. She holds a National Association of Elementary School Principal Mentor Certification and is a Certified Gallup-Strengths Coach.

She is a proud member of Delta Sigma Theta Sorority, Incorporated, International Association of Women (IAW), Sisters4Sisters Network, Inc, an Official Member of the Forbes Coaches Council, the American Business Women's Association (ABWA) and the Professional Women of Winston-Salem.

www.ingramcontent.com/pod-product-compliance
Lightning Source LLC
Chambersburg PA
CBHW070551170426
43201CB00012B/1799